HOR IS KIAS = Veg

TOU O............

D0626483

ESSENTIAL
ATHENS

Original text by Mike Gerrard
Updated by Mike Gerrard

© Automobile Association Developments Limited 2008
First published 2008
Reprinted Jan 2009

ISBN: 978-0-7495-6170-3

Published by AA Publishing, a trading name of Automobile Association Developments
Limited, whose registered office is Fanum House, Basing View, Basingstoke,
Hampshire RG21 4EA. Registered number 1878835.

Colour separation: MRM Graphics Ltd
Printed and bound in Italy by Printer Trento S.r.l.

A04024
Maps in this title produced from map data © New Holland Publishing (South Africa)
(Pty) Ltd. 2006
Transport map © Communicarta Ltd, UK

About this book

Symbols are used to denote the following categories:

- ✚ map reference to maps on cover
- ✉ address or location
- ☎ telephone number
- ⏱ opening times
- ✋ admission charge
- 🍴 restaurant or café on premises or nearby
- Ⓜ nearest underground train station
- 🚌 nearest bus/tram route
- 🚆 nearest overground train station
- ⛴ nearest ferry stop
- ✈ nearest airport
- ❓ other practical information
- ℹ tourist information office
- ➤ indicates the page where you will find a fuller description

This book is divided into six sections.

The essence of Athens pages 6–19
Introduction; Features; Food and Drink; Short Break including the 10 Essentials

Planning pages 20–33
Before You Go; Getting There; Getting Around; Being There

Best places to see pages 34–55
The unmissable highlights of any visit to Athens

Best things to do pages 56–71
Good places to have lunch; top activities; stunning views and more

Exploring pages 72–157
The best places to visit in Athens, organized by area

Excursions pages 158–181
Places to visit out of town

Maps
All map references are to the maps on the covers. For example, the Acropolis has the reference ✚ 17J – indicating the grid square in which it is to be found

Admission prices
Inexpensive (under €4)
Moderate (€5–€8)
Expensive (over €8)

Hotel prices
Price are per room per night in high season: € budget (under €100); €€ moderate (€100–€150); €€€ expensive (over €150)

Restaurant prices
Price for a three-course meal per person without drinks or service: € budget (under €15); €€ moderate (€15–€25); €€€ expensive (over €25)

Contents

BEST THINGS TO DO

56 – 71

EXPLORING...

72 – 157

EXCURSIONS

158 – 181

The essence of...

ACROPOLIS

Arriving in Athens and seeing the Acropolis standing proud above the city cannot fail to lift the spirits, for the first-time and return visitor alike. Athens is an ancient city with many layers of history, most of them on show in the National Archaeological Museum, but it is also a modern city where history is still very much in the making: the 2004 Olympic Games had a huge effect in modernizing the city, which continues to this day. Your visit will be all the richer if you consider the present and the future, as well as the past. But what a past it has!

features

Many visitors to Athens just see the traffic, and not the people. Athens is indeed far too busy and noisy, and bedevilled with smog, and too hot in August. And yet, and yet...the city has made and continues to make great efforts to improve the centre. There are ongoing schemes to restrict traffic access and expand the several large and pleasant new pedestrianized areas. The once-drab Omonia Square is considerably smarter, new boutique hotels continue to open and Athens now boasts several Michelin-star restaurants. Monuments like the Acropolis stand aloof from the changes, however, and Byzantine churches ignore the hubbub. The National Archaeological Museum remains one of the finest museums in the world. And the Athenians remain resolutely themselves, at home in their city, as any visitor could be if he or she remembers to look for the little human touches.

WET OR DRY

● It rains in Athens for about 100 days each year. However, all that rain only amounts to 400mm (15.5 inches) per annum, falling mainly in the winter and hardly at all from July to September. July and August are equally hot, with an average temperature of 32°C (90°F). The coldest month is January, averaging 12°C (54°F).

POPULATION

● Almost four million people live in the Greater Athens area. This is a third of the Greek population, which is about 11 million. In the late 19th century, the population was only 124,000.

AREA

● The Greater Athens area covers 427sq km (165sq miles), and is mostly surrounded by natural boundaries. The Aegean Sea is to the south, while to the northeast, northwest, east and west are the hill and mountain ranges of Pentelikon, Parnes, Hymettus and Aegaleos respectively. The highest is the Parnes range, rising to 1,413m (4,636ft).

INITIALLY ATHENS

● Visitors will regularly see certain sets of initials in Athens, among them the following:

EHS The urban railway service
ELPA The Touring and Automobile Club of Greece
ELTA The Post Office
EOT Tourist information offices (**NTOG** overseas)
KTEL The private bus service
OASA/ETHEL The public bus service
OSE The Railway Organisation
OTE The telephone service

food & drink

It's easy to eat a poor meal in Athens – certain places in the Plaka spring to mind – but it is just as easy to make every meal a memorable one. Some places are low on sophistication, but great on atmosphere, price and hearty traditional food. There are hundreds of reliable medium-priced places too, and an ever-increasing number of new restaurants with chefs attempting to blend traditional Greek cooking with the latest world trends.

WHEN TO EAT

Greeks tend to eat late, and seldom eat light. Restaurants are usually open from about noon onwards for lunch, and from 7pm for supper, but that is usually to catch the tourist trade – owners know that Athenians will not be out in force for some time. Many of the day's specials are prepared

in the morning or at lunchtime, and a dish such as moussaka may be served lukewarm rather than piping hot – but that is the Greek way. If you like hot food, eat early or order something that you know has to be freshly prepared, like grilled meat or fish.

FOR STARTERS

Everyone knows about *taramasalata* and *tzatziki*, but there are many other enticing starters. A dip made from aubergines, *melitzanasalata*, is delicious, while a plate of feta cheese is another Greek favourite. Deep-fried, when it is called *saganaki*, it is excellent. Florina peppers are sweet red peppers, marinated, baked and served cold: and they look as good as they taste!

WHAT TO DRINK

The Greek aperitif is ouzo, an aniseed-flavoured clear spirit that turns milky with water. Ouzo is always served with a glass of water, and sometimes with a small plate of nibbles too. Greeks tend to drink ouzo neat, with a sip of water afterwards, rather than mix the two.

The Greeks don't drink a lot of wine, even though the country is renowned for its unique resinated white wine, retsina. Athenians out for a meal may well have beer and soft drinks. More recently, however, encouraged by the demands of visitors and the increasing sophistication of Athenian palates, Greek wine-makers have responded with an improvement in quality and some award-winning products. Look for labels with names such as Boutari, Tsantalis, Kourtakis and Domaine Carras, the country's leading producers. Greek grapes have unfamiliar names, so ask if they are sweet or dry.

After a meal it is common to drink a Greek brandy, although this is often done in a bar or at a pastry shop rather than in the restaurant. The brand name Metaxa is so dominant that it has become synonymous with the word 'brandy'. If you like your brandy smooth it is wise to choose the most expensive type, the 7-star Metaxa. Fewer stars generally mean a rougher drink.

short break

If you only have a short time to visit Athens, or would like to get a really complete picture of the city, here are the essentials:

● **Visit the Acropolis** (➤ 38–39), one of the world's greatest buildings. To beat the crowds, be the first one there when it opens.

● **See the National Archaeological Museum** (➤ 40–41) – allow at least a half-day.

● **Stroll the Plaka at night** (▶ 91–110), when the locals and tourists throng the mostly traffic-free streets, enjoying the atmosphere and a good evening meal.

● **See the Sunday morning flea market** around Monastiraki (▶ 50–51), all bustle and bargains, and the kind of place about which they say, 'if you can't buy it here then it can't be bought'.

● **Eat in a busy taverna,** such as the Sigalas (▶ 124) on Monastiraki Square, especially for a weekend lunch.

● **Eat in a good restaurant.** Splash out on a meal at one of the many fine eating places in Athens. You don't have to stick to *souvlaki* and Greek salad.

● **Experiment with** the new wave of

good Greek wines (▶ 14). If you see a wine list with unfamiliar names, ask the staff about them.

● **Enter a church** to see the icons and sit a while, watching Athenians come and go. It's also an escape from the noise and traffic.

● **Linger over a coffee or an ouzo.** Have a coffee in the daytime or a pre-dinner ouzo, while watching the Athenian world go by.

● **See some of the lesser-known museums:** the Museum of Cycladic Art (▶ 46–47) is stunning, the Museum of Greek Musical Instruments (▶ 98) terrific fun, and many of the smaller museums, like the Benáki Museum (▶ 44–45), contain items of exquisite beauty.

Planning

Before you go

WHEN TO GO

JAN	FEB	MAR	APR	MAY	JUN	JUL	AUG	SEP	OCT	NOV	DEC
9°C	11°C	12°C	16°C	20°C	24°C	27°C	28°C	24°C	20°C	15°C	14°C
48°F	52°F	54°F	61°F	68°F	75°F	81°F	82°F	75°F	68°F	59°F	57°F

High season   Low season

Athens is best avoided in August, and increasingly in July too, as there have been several heat waves during these months in recent years, sometimes causing fires around the city. Summer smog used to be a problem in some places. While it does still happen, it's nowhere near as bad as it used to be, thanks to anti-pollution measures, particularly attemps to cut down the number of cars in the city centre.

April/May and September/October are good times to visit, when it is usually dry with clear blue skies. It can get cold and wet in winter, but this is the Mediterranean and winter can also see beautifully warm and clear days when visitors, though not locals, can find themselves walking around in shorts and T-shirts.

WHAT YOU NEED

		UK	Germany	USA	Netherlands	Spain
●	Required					
○	Suggested					
▲	Not required					

Some countries require a passport to remain valid for a minimum period (usually at least six months) beyond the date of entry – contact their consulate or embassy or your travel agency for details.

	UK	Germany	USA	Netherlands	Spain
Passport/National Identity Card	●	●	●	●	●
Visa (Regulations can change – check before booking your trip)	▲	▲	▲	▲	▲
Onward or Return Ticket	▲	▲	▲	▲	▲
Health Inoculations	○	○	○	○	○
Health Documentation (➤ 23, Health Insurance)	●	●	▲	●	●
Travel Insurance	●	●	●	●	●
Driving Licence (National or International)	●	●	●	●	●
Car Insurance Certificate (if own car)	●	●	●	●	●
Car Registration Document (if own car)	●	●	●	●	●

WEBSITES

www.athenstourism.gr

www.gnto.gr

www.greektourism.com

http://athensguide.com

www.athensinfoguide.com

www.culture.gr

TOURIST OFFICES AT HOME

In the UK

National Tourist
Organisation of Greece
(NTOG)
4 Conduit Street
London W1R 0DJ
☎ 020 7734 7997
www.gnto.co.uk

In the USA

National Tourist
Organisation of Greece
(NTOG)
645 Fifth Avenue
New York
NY 10022
☎ 212/421-5777
www.greektourism.com

In Canada

GNTO/EOT
1170 place du Frère
André
Suite 300
Montréal
Quebec
H3B 3C6
☎ 514/871-1535
www.greektourism.com

HEALTH INSURANCE

Visitors from the European Union (EU) are entitled to reciprocal state
medical care in Greece and should take with them a European Health
Insurance Card (EHIC), available from post offices. However, private
medical insurance is also recommended.

Dental treatment must be paid for by all visitors. Hotels can normally
provide names of local English-speaking dentists; alternatively ask your
consulate. Private medical insurance is strongly advised to cover the cost
of dental treatment.

TIME DIFFERENCES

GMT	Athens	Germany	USA (NY)	Netherlands	Spain
12 noon	2PM	1PM	7AM	1PM	1PM

Athens is two hours ahead of Greenwich Mean Time (GMT+2). The clocks
go forward one hour on the last Sunday in March, and back one hour on
the last Sunday in October.

NATIONAL HOLIDAYS

1 Jan *New Year's Day*
6 Jan *Epiphany*
Feb/Mar *Greek 'Carnival' season, three weeks before the beginning of Lent*
Feb/Mar *Shrove Monday (41 days pre-Easter)*
25 Mar *Independence Day*
Mar/Apr *Good Friday, Easter Monday*
1 May *Labour Day*

May/Jun *Whit Monday (50 days after Easter)*
15 Aug *Feast of the Assumption of the Blessed Virgin Mary*
28 Oct *Óchi Day*
25/26 Dec *Christmas*

Restaurants and tourist shops may well stay open on these days, but museums will be closed.

A number of Greek celebrations and festivities are determined by the Orthodox calendar, and could be held at different times each year. It is important, therefore, to check before travelling, especially if you wish to join in – or avoid – major festivals, such as Easter.

WHAT'S ON WHEN
January
The Feast of St Basil (1 Jan): church services.
Epiphany (6 Jan): when priests bless baptismal fonts.

March
Independence Day (25 Mar): celebrates the start of the revolt against Turkish domination and features speeches and celebrations in Syntagma Square.

February/March
Carnival (Karnaváli) is not celebrated as widely in Greece as elsewhere in the world, though in Athens you may find impromptu music sessions in the streets, with children wearing costumes and hitting people on the head with plastic hammers. The Pláka becomes packed with Athenians. The carnival takes place during the three weeks prior to Lent, with the biggest celebrations on the Sunday immediately before the start of Lent – seven weeks before Easter weekend.

March/April
Easter is by far the biggest and most important event in the Greek calendar, and it is well worth visiting Athens and other parts of Greece to

witness the festivities. Churches will be open prior to Easter weekend as people prepare for the festivities. The bier on which Christ's body will be laid is decorated with flowers, and on Friday evening is carried through the streets. On Easter Saturday evening the main church service takes place, climaxing at midnight. On Easter Sunday families get together for big celebrations.

May
Labour Day (1 May): in common with many other countries, there are traditional workers' parades.

May/Jun
Whit (Feast of the Holy Spirit): seven weeks (50 days) after the Greek Easter, Whit Sunday and Monday are also celebrated. Monday is a national holiday with parades and parties.

Summer
Summer brings the annual Athens Festival. A special box office for tickets to events opens in the early summer in the arcade at Stadiou 4 ☎ 322-1459. Mon–Sat 8:30–2, 5–7, Sun 10:30–1.
In July and August is the *Daphni Wine Festival*.

August
Feast of the Assumption (15 Aug): when Greeks make an effort to return to their home villages, and ferries are often full. This is therefore a bad time to be travelling to or from Athens.

October
Óchi Day (28 Oct): in honour of the Greek leader, General Metaxas, who allegedly gave a one-word response of 'Óchi' (No) to Mussolini's request that his troops be allowed to pass through Greece. Syntagma is the focal point, but parades are held throughout the city.

December
The Greek year winds down with *Christmas and New Year's Eve*, though these are not as important to the Greeks as Easter.

Getting there

BY AIR

Eleftherios Venizelos International Airport, Athens

27km (17 miles) to city centre

🚆 N/A

🚌 1 hour

🚗 1 hour

International flights arrive at Eleftherios Venizelos Athens International Airport. This includes Olympic Airways, the national carrier of Greece, numerous other scheduled airlines from all over the world and some European budget airlines. This bright new airport was opened for the 2004 Olympic Games, and is connected to the city centre with a cheap and efficient metro line. There are also bus connections, with both bus and metro being options if you are travelling to the port at Piraeus to catch a ferry. Taxis are also available outside the airport. A helpful branch of the Greek National Tourism Organisation can be found in the Arrivals lounge.

Getting around

PUBLIC TRANSPORT

Internal flights Domestic flights are operated by Olympic Airways and other carriers. There are connections at Athens to several provincial airports and to the Greek Islands. Domestic tickets on

Olympic Airways are non-transferable, and a no-smoking policy is operated on all their internal flights.

Trains There are two railway stations in Athens, Peloponnisou (☎ 513 1601) for the Peloponnese and nearby Larissis (☎ 823 7741) for lines north. Services are more restricted than in other countries, due partly to the terrain and partly to the well-established excellent bus service. For timetable information ☎ 145/6/7.

Metro The metro system has three lines. M1 runs from Piraeus in the southwest to Kifissia in the north. M2 runs from the northwest to Syntagma Square and then on to the southeast of the city. M3 runs from Monastiraki through Syntagma Square and then northeast all the way to the airport. Journeys are cheap, based on a zone system. Trains run every 3 to 5 minutes from 5am to midnight.

Buses Despite a huge network, this is not the best way to get around Athens. Tickets (€0.50 or €0.70) are valid for one journey and must be bought in advance from a booth near the bus stop, or certain kiosks and shops. They must then be punched on the machine on board, though buses can be so crowded it is impossible to reach the machine.

Ferries/hydrofoils The main ferry port in Athens is Piraeus, which runs services to mainland towns and certain islands. There are several different harbours here, some distance apart, so be sure to check from which harbour your service departs. Timetables can be obtained from offices of the NTOG.

TAXIS

Taxi meters should be switched on when you enter. There's a minimum fare with an additional cost per kilometre in the city and per piece of luggage. Book in advance if your journey is important. There is also a taxi-sharing scheme to help reduce traffic congestion.

FARES AND TICKETS

Although you can buy tickets for individual journeys, you can also buy a €1 ticket, which is valid for 90 minutes on all public transport in the city centre. A better option is to buy a 1-day pass for €3, which is also valid in the city centre and on metro, bus, trolleybus and tram. The 24-hour period only starts when you validate the card, so it can be spread across two days. The equivalent pass for one week costs €10.

DRIVING

- Speed limit on motorways: 120kph (74mph); outside built-up areas: 80kph (50mph); in built-up areas: 50kph (31mph)
- Seat belts must be worn in front seats at all times and in rear seats where fitted. Children under 10 are not allowed in front seats.
- It is best not to drink and drive. Penalties are severe.
- Petrol *(venzini)* usually comes in five grades: super *(sooper)*, regular *(apli)*, unleaded *(amolyvdhi)*, super unleaded *(sooper amolyvdhi)* and diesel *(petrelaio)*. Petrol stations are normally open 7–7 (closed Sun) though larger ones open 24 hours. Most take credit cards. There are few stations in remote areas.
- If you break down driving your own car then the Automobile and Touring Club of Greece (ELPA) (☎ 779-1615) provide 24-hour road assistance (☎ 104). If the car is hired, follow the instructions given in the documentation; most of the international rental firms provide a rescue service.

CAR RENTAL

Most leading car rental companies have offices in Athens, many along Syngrou. Most also have desks at the airport. It is expensive, and accident rates are high. The minimum age for car rental ranges from 21 to 25.

Being there

TOURIST OFFICE
Greek National Tourist Office
Amalias 26
☎ 331-0392
🕐 Mon–Fri 9–8, Sat–Sun 10–7
There is also an office in the Arrivals
hall of the airport ☎ 331-0445.

MONEY
The currency of Greece is the euro (€). Euro notes are issued in
denominations of 5, 10, 20, 50, 100, 200 and 500 euros, coins of 1 and 2
euros and 1, 2, 5, 10 and 50 cents; 100 cents = €1. Travellers' cheques are
accepted by most hotels, shops and restaurants. There are banks and
ATMs on almost every street in Athens, along with money exchange
offices where travellers' cheques and cash can be exchanged and
advances on credit cards obtained.

TIPS/GRATUITIES

Yes ✓ No ✗		
Restaurants (service not inc.)	✓	10–15%
Cafés/bars (service not inc.)	✓	change
Tour guides	✓	€2
Hairdressers	✓	change
Taxis	✓	change
Chambermaids	✓	€1
Porters	✓	€1
Cloakroom attendants	✓	change
Toilets	✓	change

POSTAL AND INTERNET SERVICES
Post offices *(takhydhromio)* are distinguished by a yellow OTE sign. They
are normally open morning shop hours only, except for a couple of main
branches . Queues can be long so if you only want stamps,
(ghramatósima), try kiosks or shops selling postcards.

Internet cafés are widespread in Athens, and most of the better hotels have modem ports in their guest rooms. Wireless access is slowly becoming more commonplace, but not to the extent it is in most other European capitals.

TELEPHONES

Most public telephones now accept only phonecards, available from kiosks and some shops in units of 100, 200, 500 and 1,000. Otherwise, use the phone available at most roadside kiosks: your call is metred and you pay in cash. Some hotels, restaurants and bars have phones accepting coins. For the operator dial 132 or 131.

International dialling codes
From Athens to:
UK: 00 44
Germany: 00 49
USA & Canada: 00 1
Netherlands: 00 31
Spain: 00 34

Emergency telephone numbers
Police 100
Fire 199
Ambulance 166
Tourist Police 171 (Athens) 902-5992 (outside Athens)
Visitor Emergency Assistance 112

EMBASSIES AND CONSULATES

UK ☎ 727-2600
Germany ☎ 728-5111
USA ☎ 721-2951

Netherlands ☎ 725-4900
Spain ☎ 921-3123

HEALTH ADVICE

Sun advice The sunniest months are July and August, with daytime temperatures well up into the 30s (top 80s, low 90s °F and often over 40°C (104°F). Avoid the midday sun and use a strong sunblock. Don't underestimate the dehydration effects of walking around sightseeing – drink lots of water.

Drugs Prescription and non-prescription drugs and medicines are available from pharmacies *(farmakia)*, distinguished by a large green cross. Note that codeine is banned in Greece and you can be fined for carrying it.

Safe water Tap water is perfectly safe to drink, but bottled water is widely available.

PERSONAL SAFETY

Greece is one of the safest countries in the world and you are unlikely to experience any problems. Nevertheless, Athens is a city like any other, with its share of impoverished migrants and drug addicts desperate for cash, so exercise the usual precautions:

- Beware of pickpockets in markets, tourist sights or crowded places.
- Avoid walking alone in unlit streets at night.

ELECTRICITY

The power supply is 220 volts AC, 50 Hz. Sockets accept two-pin round plugs, so an adaptor is needed for most non-Continental European appliances and a transformer for appliances operating on other voltages.

OPENING HOURS

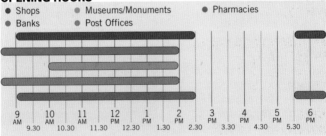

- Shops
- Banks
- Museums/Monuments
- Post Offices
- Pharmacies

| 9 AM | 10 AM | 11 AM | 12 PM | 1 PM | 2 PM | 3 PM | 4 PM | 5 PM | 6 PM |
| 9.30 | 10.30 | 11.30 | 12.30 | 1.30 | 2.30 | 3.30 | 4.30 | 5.30 | |

Pharmacies normally open on weekdays only. Monasteries open during daylight hours; churches are often open all day, though some may open early morning and evenings only. Opening hours are flexible, especially those of museums, which change annually, if only by 15 minutes or so. Longer hours operate in summer, so check in case of restricted hours if travelling between October and Easter. Four post offices open late: Metropoleos, Syntagma; Aïolou 100, Omonia Square; Metropoleos Square; Arrivals Terminal, Athens Airport. Mon–Fri until 8; Sat, Sun mornings (not Metropoleos).

THE GREEK ALPHABET

The Greek alphabet cannot be transliterated into other languages in a straightforward way. This can lead to variations in romanised spellings of Greek words and placenames. It also leads inevitably to inconsistencies, especially when comparing different guide books, leaflets and signs. However, the differences rarely make any name unrecognisable. The language looks complex, but it is worth memorising the alphabet to help with signs, destinations etc.

Alpha	Αα	short a, as in hat
Beta	Ββ	v sound
Gamma	Γγ	guttural g sound
Delta	Δδ	soft th, as in father
Epsilon	Εε	short e
Zita	Ζζ	z sound
Eta	Ηη	long e, as in feet
Theta	Θθ	hard th, as in think
Iota	Ιι	short i, as in hit
Kappa	Κκ	k sound
Lambda	Λλ	l sound
Mu	Μμ	m sound
Nu	Νν	n sound
Xi	Ξξ	x or ks sound
Omicron	Οο	short o, as in pot
Pi	Ππ	p sound
Rho	Πρ	r sound
Sigma	Σσ	s sound
	ς	(at end of word)
Tau	Ττ	t sound
Upsilon	Υυ	ee, or y as in funny
Phi	Φφ	f sound
Chi	Χχ	guttural ch, as in loch
Psi	Ψψ	ps, as in chops
Omega	Ωω	long o, as in bone

LANGUAGE

The Greek language can look daunting to the visitor, and certainly sounds it because the Greeks speak with a machine-gun rapidity. Although transliterations vary, learning the alphabet will help with road signs and bus destinations, as romanisations will vary, but not a great deal. It is also worth trying to learn a few basic courtesy phrases; the Greeks themselves know how difficult their language is for foreigners and appreciate the visitor's attempts to learn it.

WORDS AND PHRASES

yes/no	*neh/óchi*	excuse me	*signómi*
please	*parakaló*	you're welcome	*parakaló*
thank you	*efharistó*	how are you?	*pos iseh?*
hello	*ya sas*	do you speak	*miláte angliká?*
goodbye	*adío*	English?	
good morning	*kali méra*	I don't understand	*dhen katalavéno*
good evening	*kali spéra*	how much?	*póso?*
goodnight	*kali níchta*	open	*aniktós*
where is...?	*pou eínai...?*	closed	*klistó*

hotel	*xenothokhío*	room service	*sérvis thomatíou*
bed and breakfast	*thomátio meh proinó*	chambermaid	*kamaryéra*
single room	*monóklino*	bath/shower	*bányo/doos*
double room	*diklino*	toilet	*tooaléta*
one person	*éna átomo*	balcony	*balkóni*
one night	*mia níkhta*	key	*klithí*
reservation	*mia krátisi*	sea view	*vthéa ti thálasa*

bank/exchange office	*trápeza/sarafiko*	travellers' cheque	*taxithiotikí epitayi*
post office	*takhithromío*	credit card	*pistotikí kárta*
coin	*kérma*	change	*resta*
banknote	*khartonómisma*	foreign currency	*khartonómismes*
cheque	*epitayí*		*xénes*

café/bar	*café/bar*	main course	*kírio piáto*
breakfast	*proinó*	dessert	*glikisma*
lunch/dinner	*yévma/mesimeriano*	bill	*logariasmó*
table	*trapézi*	beer/wine	*bíra/krasí*
waiter/waitress	*garsón/garsóna*	water	*neró*
starter	*proto piáto*	coffee	*café*

airport	*aerothrómio*	ferry	*féribot*
train/bus	*treno/leoforío*	single ticket	*apló*
station	*stathmós*	return ticket	*isitirio metepistrofís*
boat/port	*plio/limáni*	car/petrol	*aftokínito/venzíni*
ticket	*isitírio*	bus stop	*stási leoforiou*

Best places to see

1 Agorá

After the Acropolis, the market place of ancient Athens is the other 'must see'. It features some good remains and a fine, small museum.

Imagine the Agorá filled with stalls and shops, its streets and squares packed with buyers and sellers. It helps to buy a plan or to consult one of the information boards dotted around the site. The area was first used as a market place in about the 6th century BC; before that it was a cemetery. The site was at the heart of Athenian life for centuries, along

with the Acropolis, which rises behind it. In fact, a good overview of the Agorá can be had from the Acropolis, or from the neighbouring Areopagos (► 93).

At ground level the foundations of many buildings are still evident, with signs in English for some of them. Two buildings dominate opposite ends of the site. One is the Temple of Hephaistos (► 100), and the other the Stoa Atallou (Stoa of Attalos), which contains the Agorá's excellent little museum. The Stoa is a two-storey arcade, first built in the 2nd century BC, which has been immaculately restored by the American School of Archaeology in Athens, giving us a rare opportunity to see what Greek buildings of the period actually looked like. Inside, the museum is full of quirky finds that bring old Athens to life: a child's commode, a fragment of a library rule-book, a machine used for the selection of officials. Between the museum and the Acropolis is another restored building, the Church of the Holy Apostles (► 92).

✚ 16H ✉ Adrianou 24 ☎ 321-0185 ⊘ Tue–Sun 8–7:30, Mon 11–7:30; closes 5pm Nov–Mar. Closed public hols ♿ Expensive. Combined ticket to this and 5 other sites Ⓜ Thissio/Monastiraki

2 Akrópoli (Acropolis)

Acropolis means 'upper city', and refers to the outcrop of rock that rises above the city around which Athens was founded and later flourished.

There are several buildings on top of the Acropolis. All were part of a building boom instigated by Pericles – ruler and military leader of Athens – in the 5th century BC. The finest of these is the Parthenon. The city's greatest sculptors worked on the building, achieving a consistently pleasing whole under the guidance of the greatest sculptor of them all, Pheidias. Despite the apparent geometrical symmetry, there are no straight lines in the Parthenon's construction, as all its floors, columns and friezes taper very subtly to create a visual harmony. It is built of a marble which contains some iron, and this contributes to the stunning golden glow that the building develops in a good sunset. It is also a thrilling sight at night, when it is illuminated.

Several other buildings make up the Acropolis, including the Propylaia, which is on the left as you enter and was the original imposing

gateway. The small Temple of Athena Nike (Athena, Bringer of Victory) was demolished by the Turks in 1686, but lovingly restored in the 19th century. The Eréchtheio, on the far side of the Sacred Way from the Parthenon, is said to have been the place where Athena brought forth the first olive tree. At the time of writing the Acropolis Museum was closed while its contents were being transferred to the New Acropolis Museum (▶ 80). It is expected to be used in the future for changing exhibitions.

✛ 17J ☎ 321-4172 ◉ Daily 8–7:30 (closes 5pm Nov–Mar). Closed public hols 🖐 Expensive. Combined ticket to this and 5 other sites ◙ Akropoli ❓ Sound and light show, seating and tickets on the Pnýka

3 Ethnikó Archeologikó Mouseío (National Archaeological Museum)

This is one of the world's great museums, ranking alongside the British Museum in London and the Louvre in Paris.

Highlights include beautiful frescoes from houses on Thíra (Santorini), which were contemporaneous with the Cretan Minoan civilization before being engulfed in the island's massive earthquake. Elsewhere are treasures from Mycenae, including the gold mask which caused archaeologist Heinrich Schliemann to declare, 'I have gazed upon the face of Agamemnon'. Many of the statues in the museum will be familiar, including a magnificent figure of Poseidon about to throw his trident, while on a more delicate scale the 'Jockey-boy' of Artemission shows a young boy encouraging his horse with great urgency and grace.

If time is limited, the following 'highlights' tour may help. On going through the doors to the left of the main entrance hall, walk straight ahead as far as you can go, turn right, and a few rooms ahead of you is Poseidon. At the far end of that gallery, turn right and walk to the marbled central hall where the 'Jockey-

boy' bronze statue is displayed. The stairs to the upper floor are now on your left. In the room to the left at the foot of the stairs is a marvellous collection of bronzes, including a rampant satyr, familiar from risqué Greek postcards, yet so tiny in actuality you may not notice it. At the top of the stairs, straight ahead up a few more steps, is the collection of delicate frescoes from Santorini, dating from about 1500BC. Walking back down the stairs you will find the temporary exhibition halls to your left. If, however, you walk straight ahead you will come to the Mycenean Hall, containing the great golden treasures from that ancient palace complex. As well as the renowned death masks (contemporaneous with the Thíra frescoes), make sure you also see the bull's head with its golden horns, a breathtakingly beautiful creation.

Rooms 7 to 35 concentrate on sculpture, rooms 36 to 39 house a collection of bronzes, and 40 and 41 display impressive artefacts from ancient Egypt.

If you want to know more about the collection, guides can be hired for personal tours in English, French, German, Italian and Spanish; you can ask for short or long tours. Booking is at the entrance next to the stairs leading to the basement café, where you will also find a display of casts and reproductions from the collection for sale.

🟰 6B ✉ 28 Oktovriou (Patissíon) 44 ☎ 821-7717
🕐 Apr–Oct Mon 1–7, Tue–Sun 8–7; Nov–Mar Tue–Sun 8–5. Closed public hols and Mon in winter. Gift shop Tue–Sat 8:30–2:30. Closed Sun and Mon 🖐 Expensive
🍴 Café (€€) 🚇 Omonia ❓ Guided tours in several languages

4 Lykavitós (Lycabettus Hill)

The highest hill in Athens at 278m (912ft), Lycabettus dominates the city almost as much as the Acropolis, of which there is an excellent view from the top.

Lycabettus was once well outside the city boundaries, because, as recently as the 19th century, Athens was merely a small cluster of houses around the Acropolis. It is hard to imagine that today, as you gaze out from the hilltop and see the modern metropolis sprawling before you, all the way to Piraeus on the coast. Some of the offshore islands in the Saronic Gulf can also be seen, including Aegina (► 161) on a clear day.

To the north is Mount Parnes. It's a stiff climb to get to the top of this chalk outcrop, but a very pleasant one – through pine-scented woods, often filled with butterflies, and you might even see a few wild tortoises. There are several routes up, plenty of benches on which to take a breather, a café half-way up and another at the very top. Here, too, is the small, whitewashed 19th-century chapel of

Ágios Geórgios (St George), whose feast is celebrated on 23 April.

Below the summit, on the far side, is the modern, open-air Lycabettus Theatre, where concerts are frequently held: dance, jazz, classical and rock. It is also possible to take a funicular to the top and back; this stays open till 11:45pm reflecting the popularity of the hill at night. This is the perfect place for a late-night coffee or brandy, with the illuminated city spread out at your feet.

➕ 10C 🚡 Funicular from the corner of Aristippou and Ploutarchou daily 9am–11:45pm ✋ Hill free, open access; funicular moderate 🍴 Cafés (€€€) 🚇 Evangelismos 🚌 023

5 Mouseío Benáki (Benáki Museum)

This neoclassical mansion, built in 1867 but extended and refurbished several times over the years, houses an amazing collection of Greek and Egyptian items.

The exhibits, and the house in which they are displayed, belonged to an Alexandrian Greek cotton trader, Antoine Emmanuel Benáki (1873–1954). Over a period of 35 years he amassed a splendid selection of artefacts, which he eventually gave to the Greek state for display in a museum.

The mansion was thoroughly renovated in the late 1990s to create a fine backdrop for the artefacts. Thirty thousand pieces illustrate the daily life in Greece from ancient times to the 20th

century. The collection incorporates paintings (including two by El Greco), jewellery from Mycenae, ceramics, icons, clothing and Greek folk art, such as bridal cushions, traditional clothing and decorative items. Lord Byron's writing desk is one of the many items from the War of Independence, along with other historical objects. The Egyptian collection is also fascinating. Early Coptic textiles and jewellery give an impression of the wealth of artistic talent found within this still-thriving community. Don't miss the café-restaurant at the top, with a terrace that offers fine views and the perfect place to take a break after the time you will no doubt spend walking around this wonderful collection.

🚼 9E ✉ Koumbari 1 ☎ 67-1000
🕓 Mon, Wed, Fri–Sat 9–5, Thu 9–midnight, Sun 9–3 💷 Expensive
🍴 Café (€€) 🚇 Evangelismos
🚌 234

6 Mouseío Kykladikís Téchnis (Museum of Cycladic Art)

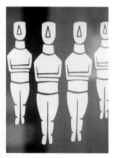

This first-class modern museum houses the remarkable private collection of Nikolas P Goulandris, a shipowner and patron of the arts.

The displays span many centuries of ancient Greek art – vases, glassware and other items – but the central exhibits are the beautiful artefacts from the Cycladic civilisation of 3000–2000BC. The statues are especially memorable – the figures seem to float in their display cabinets as subtle lighting brings out their shape and texture. It will be a rare visitor who is not tempted to take home a copy from the attractive museum shop.

The actual Cycladic items only take up one of the four floors in the main building, and the rooms are

quite small – just one main room on each floor. The others are given over to a collection of Bronze Age items, one from the Mycenean period, and a remarkable collection of beautiful Cypriot antiquities, the largest one in Greece.

On the corner of Irodotou and Vasilissis

Sofias is the entrance to the new wing (added in 1992) of the Cycladic Museum, joined to the main building by a glass-covered walkway. This wing is as interesting for the building that houses it as for its contents. It was designed by and was the home of the German architect Ernst Ziller, the man also responsible for the Olympic Stadium, the Presidential Palace and Heinrich Schliemann's house on Panepistimiou. Some rooms of the museum display furniture and watercolours, giving an impression of the mansion's appearance when Ziller lived in it during the late 19th century. Other rooms contain an extension of the main Cycladic collection. There is a shop downstairs, and space upstairs for temporary exhibitions.

➕ 11E ✉ Neofytou Douka 4 ☎ 722-8321, 724-9706 (shop)
🕐 Mon, Thu–Fri 10–4, Wed 10–8 (summer only),
Sat 10–3. Closed Tue, Sun, public hols 👎 Moderate
🍴 Café (€€) Ⓜ Evangelismos 🚌 234

7 Panathinaikó Stádio (Panathenian Stadium)

For sheer, simple grace, the beauty of this stone athletics stadium, within sight of the equally graceful Acropolis, is hard to beat.

This stadium was built in 1896 when the Olympic Games were revived and fittingly held in their original home. Many Greeks were disappointed at not being awarded the 1996 Olympics, though they did eventually get the 2004 Games. The 1896 stadium is also named after the Panathenaic Stadium, where contests were held on this site from the 4th century BC onwards. The Olympic stadium follows the same plan as the ancient stadium, which was described by the geographer Pausanias in the 2nd century AD. Architect Ernst Ziller, responsible for many fine late 19th-century Athenian buildings, was commissioned to design the stadium in the spirit of its predecessor.

A visit to the stadium won't take long as there is little to see other than the structure as a whole, but you may find some Athenians jogging round the track, and visitors can wander around the centre and look at the statues marking starting and finishing points. Photographers will also be tempted by the sweeping curves and repetitive lines of the 47 rows of seats, which hold up to 60,000 spectators. The seating is on three sides only, leaving the fourth open with views across to one of the few wooded areas in central Athens, a corner of the National Gardens. The Panathenian Stadium is not to be confused with the modern Olympic Stadium, which was built in 1982 in the northern suburbs.

✚ 21J ✉ Ardittou ◷ Daily sunrise–sunset ✋ Free
🚌 2, 4, 11, 12

8 Plateía Monastirakíou (Monastiraki Square)

Monastiraki Square has always been one of the city's main hubs. It may be much smaller than Omonia or Syntagma, but it's just as busy with people passing through it, day and night.

In one direction are the souvenir shops of the Plaka district, and close by are the remains of the Roman Agorá, the Ancient Agora, Hadrian's Library, the Tower of the Winds and the former mosque containing the ceramic collection of the Museum of Greek Folk Art. From here you can also head up towards the ancient Acropolis or into the new nightlife areas of Psyrri and Gazi.

For many people, though, visitors and residents alike, Monastiraki marks the start of the bustling old bazaar area of Athens. The streets west of here are filled with all kinds of shops. They are increasingly clothes and souvenir shops, of the type that can be found anywhere, but many of the old-fashioned shops still survive, selling second-hand books, old computers, pots and pans or used CDs.

The area is at its liveliest at the weekends, especially Sunday mornings, when the shops are joined by stalls, and people selling unwanted goods from blankets on the floor. Collectors of old postcards, stamps, coins and even used phone cards all mingle with the regular artisans making jewellery and other arts and crafts, who can be found around Monastiraki every day of the week. The Sunday morning market is no longer quite as big and hectic as it used to be, since parts of the streets have been smartened up, but it's still a harkback to the Athens of old, and a reminder that this is a Balkan country not too far from Asia.

✚ 17G 🚇 Thissio/Monastiraki

9 Plateía Syntágmatos (Syntagma Square)

The main square of Athens, Syntagma or Constitution Square, is one that every visitor should see – and at some point probably will.

It has gained a new lease of life as a focal point of the city since the opening of its impressive metro station in time for the 2004 Olympic Games. You don't need to use the metro in order to go into the station to admire the modern design, and the way that some of the archaeological finds that were uncovered during the station's construction have been displayed. So many finds were uncovered

ΑΚΑΙΝΗΚΕΝΗΦ
ΓΑΙΕΣΤΡΙΜΕΝ
ΝΑΦΑΝΛΝ

ΜΑΣ
Α
ΟΝ
ΛΡΑΚΙ

here, and in other construction work around the city, that the delays in finishing the various projects were severe, but the city still managed to have all the essential elements in place.

There are now several pleasant and popular cafés in the centre of Syntagma, and you can use the metro station entrances here and there to avoid crossing some of the busy main streets. On the northern side of the square stands the distinguished Grande Bretagne hotel (➤ 152), whose guests over the years have included Elizabeth Taylor, Richard Strauss and Winston Churchill. Churchill stayed here during World War II and an attempt was made on his life. The hotel was built in 1862 as an annexe to what was then the summer palace of the royal family. This is now the Voulí, or Greek Parliament Building, at the eastern side of the square. In front of it is the Tomb of the Unknown Soldier, guarded by the Greek soldiers known as the Evzones. Their Changing of the Guard ritual is a popular tourist attraction, impressively dramatic.

✚ 8E 🍴 Cafés (€€) Ⓜ Syntagma 🚌 23, 25, 230

10 Vyzantinó kai Christianíko Mouseío (Byzantine and Christian Museum)

Another of Athens' specialist collections, this is partly housed in an 1840s villa with its own courtyard, filled with flowers and orange trees.

The villa was home to the Duchesse de Plaisance, a French widow who had been married to one of Napoleon's generals and who fell in love with Greece and created this Florentine villa in what was then the outskirts of Athens.

The collection was mainly of interest to the connoisseur, but has been brought to life by the building of a new and large underground wing.

Although underground, this new set of galleries is bright and spacious, with an open-plan look. The first room outlines the story of the Byzantine Empire. Armed with this overview you can make your way through the display areas, starting with Christian art and ending with the Fall of Constantinople in 1453.

Exhibits include icons, naturally, but also many other forms of Byzantine art, such as sculptures, frescoes, jewellery, ceramics, manuscripts and embroideries. There are audio tours in Greek and other languages, and some displays for blind people to touch and experience.

✚ 11E ✉ Vasilissis Sofiás 22 ☎ 723-2178 🕐 Tue–Sun 8–7:30 ✋ Moderate Ⓜ Evangelismos 🚌 234

Best things to do

Good places to have lunch

Aerides (€)
If it's cool go upstairs and gaze at the Tower of the Winds. If sunny, there are plenty of tables outside.
✉ Markou Avriliou 3 ☎ 322-6266

Barba Yannis (€)
Serves a limited menu of good Greek dishes. Great atmosphere, popular with students.
✉ Emmanuel Benaki 94 ☎ 330-0185

Five Brothers (€)
Outdoor seating in a quiet street near the Roman Agorá.
✉ Eolou 3 ☎ 325-0088

GB Corner (€€€)

If you can't afford to stay at the Grande Bretagne hotel, at least savour the atmosphere with a meal here.

✉ Grande Bretagne Hotel, Plateía Syntagmatos ☎ 333-0000

Mikrolimano (€€€)

Innumerable fish tavernas surround this small harbour in busy Piraeus. Excellent but expensive fish. Choose a place that suits your taste and budget.

Moet & Chandon Bar (€€€)

Relax in this new chic Athens bar, with top-notch nibbles and champagne.

✉ Baby Grand Hotel, Athinas 65 ☎ 325-0900

Palia Athina (€€)

Just outside the Pláka, and one of the author's favourites for its authentic food.

✉ Nikis 46 ☎ 331-2975

O Platanos (€)

There can be few better places to eat in summer than outside here, in a quiet corner beneath a plane tree.

✉ Diogenous 4 ☎ 322-0666

Sigalas (€)

Bustling old taverna in the heart of Athens, not for gourmets but as Greek as it gets.

✉ Monastiráki 2 ☎ 321-3036

Tudor Hall Restaurant (€€€)

Great views of the Parthenon from the terrace and superb food make this a popular choice.

✉ King George Palace Hotel, Plateía Syntágmatos ☎ 322-2210

Top activities

Golf: there's an international course at Glyfada, on the coast just beyond the airport ☎ 894-6820.

Horse-riding: there are a few clubs around Athens. Contact the Hellenic Riding Club, Paradisou 18 ☎ 681-2506.

Jogging: contact the Hash House Harriers Jogging Club in Kifissia to join locals and ex-pats for a run (www.athenshash.com).

Marathon: if you want to run a marathon then you may as well cover the original route, from Marathon to Athens. This is done twice a year; details from SEGAS, Syngrou 137 ☎ 933-1113; www.athensclassicmarathon.gr.

Sailing: there are marinas, yachting and sailing clubs in Piraeus, Glyfada, Vouliagmeni and other suburbs of Athens. Information from the Hellenic Yachting Federation, Xenofondos Street ☎ 940-4825.

Sea fishing: with the Aegean on its doorstep, there are plenty of opportunities. Contact the Harbour Master's Office in Zea, Piraeus ☎ 422-6000, or the Anglers and Maritime Sports Club at Akti Moutsopoulou, also in Piraeus ☎ 451-5731.

Swimming: best beaches are at Glyfada, which is packed with

Athenians in summer. Otherwise pay to use a hotel pool, such as the Hilton.

Tennis: very popular, with courts all over the city. Try the Athens Tennis Club at Vasilissis Olgas 2 ☎ 923-2872.

Walking: with a shortage of taxis and packed public transport, you are advised to walk in Athens, and a climb up Lycabettus Hill will definitely get you fit!

Water-skiing: there are several watersports clubs with water-skiing along the beaches at Vouliagméni.

Places to take the children

Beaches

Places like Glyfada provide sea and sand, and it's easy to get to and from the city centre using buses or taxis. At Astir Beach there are plenty of watersports to amuse all the family, plus good shopping and numerous places to eat. The suburbs of Varkiza, Voula and Vouliagméni also have good beach facilities, and the area around Cape Sounion is becoming known as the Athens Riviera.

Goulandris Natural History Museum

A trip to Kifissia combines a ride on the metro with a visit to this excellent museum (➤ 168). There are displays on environmental problems and collections on Greek flora and fauna, including some of the larger birds of prey and mammals such as bears and wolves.

✉ Levidou 13 ☎ 801-5870 ⏲ Mon–Sat 9–2:30, Sun 10–2:30. Closed Aug ⓜ Kifisias

Hellenic Children's Museum

Contact the museum (➤ 94) for details of current activities. Some of the staff speak English, though advance notice for visits by non-Greek speaking children is advisable.

✉ Kydathinaíon 14 ☎ 331-2995 ⏲ Tue–Fri 10–2, Sat–Sun 10–3. Closed public hols and Jul–Aug ⓜ Syntagma

Lycabettus Hill

Kids should enjoy the trip to the top of Lycabettus Hill (➤ 42–43) on the funicular. However, they may want to come straight back down again, without allowing you time to enjoy the view.

✉ Plutarhou ⏲ Daily 9am–11:45pm

Museum of Greek Children's Art

This museum (➤ 96–97) has displays that include imaginative sculptures, as well as tables and materials for children to use.

✉ Kodrou 9 ☎ 331-2621 ⏲ Tue–Sat 10–2, Sun 11–2. Closed public hols and Aug ⓜ Syntagma

National Gardens

In addition to exploring the gardens (➤ 142) and looking for small ponds where fish and terrapins live, attractions include a Children's Library in the centre of the gardens, signposted from the main entrance on Amalias. Adults are not admitted, and there are books, toys, tapes and games in Greek, English and other languages.
🕐 Daily sunrise–sunset

Panathenian Stadium

The running track of the 1896 Panathenian Stadium (➤ 48–49) is open to anyone during the day, and children might enjoy races around the track or even up the steep seating and down again.
✉ Ardittou 🕐 Daily sunrise–sunset 🚌 4, 11, 12

Piraeus and the Islands

A good day out is to take a day trip to one or more of the Argo-Saronic islands. An early start will mean a ride on the metro to Piraeus (➤ 174–175), and then the excitement of a journey on one of the hydrofoils to Aegina, Póros, Spétses or Hydra.
🚇 Piraeus

The Planetarium

Although it's a little way out of the city centre, the fairly new Planetarium has some enjoyable shows, including programmes about the ancient Greeks with joint Greek-English voice-overs.
✉ Syngrou 387 ☎ 946 9641 🕐 Wed–Fri 5:30–8:30pm, Sat–Sun 10:30–8:30
🚌 B2, 550

Syntagma Square

The Changing of the Guard (➤ 53) is a precision routine that fascinates young and old alike. It takes place hourly on the hour, with a fuller ceremony with a marching band at 10:45 on Sunday morning, in front of the Parliament Building at the top of the square.
🚇 Syntagma

a walk around the Acropolis

Beginning in Plateía Monastirakíou, walk up Areos towards the Acropolis.

On your left is the mosque housing the Ceramic Collection of the Museum of Greek Folk Art, which is well worth a visit (➤ 114). Just beyond are the remains of Hadrian's Library (➤ 119).

At the end of Areos, turn left and then right, up Dioskouron. If in doubt at any time, walk up! At the end of Dioskouron, climb the steps which zigzag towards the Acropolis, sometimes so narrow that they seem to disappear.

On your right is the Agorá (➤ 36–37). The temple you can see is the Theseion, which gives its name to the area around it. Further on is the Areopagos, and opposite on your left the entrance to the Acropolis (➤ 38–39).

If visiting the Acropolis, turn left as you leave it to walk down the steps up which the majority of tourists climb. At the bottom, turn left along Areopagitou.

On your left stands the Odeon of Herodes Atticus (► 76–77).

To visit this theatre take the path off to the left. Otherwise, continue along the road which then passes the entrance to the Theatre of Dionysus (► 86).

Across the road on your right is the New Acropolis Museum (► 80), which is due to open some time in 2008. Cross over to visit the new museum, if it is open.

If not, continue on the left-hand side of the street and look for the small street on the left just past the statue of Lord Byron. Take Vyronos (Byron Street) up as far as Plateía Lysikrátous for the end of the walk.

Distance 2km (1.2 miles)
Time 2–3 hours with stops
Start point Plateía Monastirakíou ✚ 17G 🚇 Monastiráki
End point Plateía Lysikrátous ✚ 18J 🚇 Akropoli
Lunch/tea Diogenes (€€) ✉ Selley 3, Plateía Lysikrátous
☎ 322-4845

Stunning views

From the Acropolis
Although the view of the Parthenon on top of the Acropolis is the single most recognisable view of Athens, the views from the Acropolis are also something special. On one side you can look north across the city centre to Lycabettus Hill, and in the distance the range of hills that surround Athens. To the south the view is towards Piraeus and the sea.

From Lycabettus Hill
Lycabettus is the highest point in the city centre, so naturally provides the best views. Don't forget your camera as it's from here you will want to get your perfect shot of the Acropolis, even though it's almost certain you'll have a crane in the shot, due to the ongoing restoration works. If it's a clear day, you will be able to see down to the port of Piraeus, where the Aegean glistens in the far distance, hinting at the beckoning Greek islands beyond.

From the Pnýx

The Athenian Assembly used to meet in the amphitheatre on the side of the Pnýx hill, and it gave them an impressive view of the Parthenon on top of the nearby Acropolis. Fewer visitors make it here, which is a shame as from the Pnýx you get an excellent view of the front of the Parthenon, which makes for some good photos. Professional photographers often shoot the building from here with a telephoto lens, to get the best results.

Sunset at Cape Sounion

Apart from its historical interest, the Temple of Poseidon out at Cape Sounion also adds drama to one of the most stunning views around the city of Athens. Many people make their way out here for the sunset, and when the conditions are right the rewards are tremendous. You can see right across the bay and out to sea, with several islands visible in the near and far distance. It makes you want to be on a boat sailing out towards those romantic-looking dots of land in the distance.

Best museums

Benáki Museum
The Benáki collection of historical artefacts from all over the world
(► 44–45) is so vast that two outposts have also opened in
Athens: an Islamic Art museum and the Benáki's Pireos annexe,
which concentrates on the visual arts. It is the core collection,
though, which remains as one of Athens' finest, perhaps second
only to the National Archaeological Museum.

Byzantine and Christian Museum
A new wing, which opened in 2007, transformed this museum
(► 54–55) from a small collection of interest mainly to specialists
into one of the city's most appealing
museums. Light and spacious, despite
being underground, it gives the visitor an
in-depth understanding of the Byzantine
civilization.

Museum of Cycladic Art
Close to the Benaki Museum is this small
but beautiful collection, centred on the
graceful carvings from the Cycladic
civilisation (► 46–47).

Museum of Greek Musical Instruments
This museum (► 98) hasn't changed in
years, nor does it need to. It's an enjoyable
look at the range of musical instruments
found in Greece, with some beautifully
crafted samples on display, and the chance
to hear recordings of them through
headphones. It is simple and delightful.

National Archaeological Museum
This is the one museum without which no

visit to Athens is complete, the national collection of some of the finest items ever produced by the various Greek civilizations (➤ 40–41). That one fairly small country can produce so much wonderful art is truly impressive.

New Acropolis Museum
As this book goes to press, the new museum (➤ 80) is not yet open, but from the outside it is an imposing sight. The plans are ambitious, but those who know Athens will have little doubt that the city will achieve those ambitions and produce a spectacular new building – if not necessarily on time!

Greek dishes

The best Greek food uses the freshest ingredients: fish straight from the boat; fruit, vegetables and meat straight from the field.

- **Baklava:** sweet dessert of filo pastry, honey and nuts

- **Dolmades:** vine leaves stuffed with rice and sometimes minced meat too

- **Kalamaris or kalamarakia:** fried baby squid

- **Keftedes:** meatballs often flavoured with herbs and cumin

- **Loukoumades:** deep-fried pastries soaked in honey

- **Moussaka:** layers of potatoes, minced lamb (or veal), aubergines and béchamel sauce

- **Saganaki:** deep-fried cheese

- **Spedzofai:** spicy stew of sausage, pepper, tomatoes

- **Vriam:** ratatouille-type dish of fresh vegetables

- **Yemista:** tomatoes and/or peppers stuffed with herb-flavoured rice

Exploring

Although the area of Greater Athens covers 427sq km (165sq miles) and, like any city today, it has its sprawling suburbs, most of the visitor attractions are in a small area within the city centre, mainly within easy walking distance of each other.

Walking along some of the busy Athenian streets can be a noisy experience due to the heavy traffic, yet somehow this can help you appreciate what a remarkable city it is. Roads are diverted around little Byzantine churches, and the modern metro stations display ancient archaeological remains. The ongoing work on the smart new metro network is constantly being halted when yet more treasures are uncovered.

When you walk round Athens, you are just part of the latest layer of its long history.

Mets, Makriyianni and Koukaki

LOFOS
NYMFON

MAKRY
GIANNI

*Próto
Nekrotafío
Athinón*

If you use the Acropolis as a landmark, then this area of the city lies roughly to the south and the east of that hill. It's a part of the city more familiar to Athenians than to tourists, but that will change a little when the New Acropolis Museum opens in Makriyianni in 2008.

This is quite an upmarket suburb, as indicated by the fact that the celebrated Greek jeweller Ilias Lalaounis has his museum here, but Mets and Koukaki are both a little more down-to-earth. The main attractions are historical, such as the Temple of Olympian Zeus and the 1896 Panathenian Stadium, but you'll also find some excellent eating places and nightlife catering very much for locals rather than visitors. Which is all the more reason to pay a visit.

FILOPÁPPOU (PHILOPAPPOS)

In the Pnýx (➤ 80–81) and on top
of the Hill of the Muses (147m/482ft)
is the Monument of Philopappos.
Banished to Athens by the Romans,
Philopappos became the Roman
Consul in Athens in AD100. He was
popular here because of his
generosity and was allowed to build
this grandiose tomb on one of the
city's prime sites between AD114
and 116.

On the western slopes of
Philopappou Hill is the Théatro Filopáppou
(Philopappos Theatre), also known as the Dora
Stratou Dance Theatre. Dora Stratou was a
renowned Greek dancer, who preserved
traditional Greek dances, music and costumes,
and later founded her own dance school and
dance company, which performs flamboyant
shows here every night throughout the summer
months. To reach the theatre, take the entrance to
the Pnýx, which is opposite the Acropolis
entrance on Areopagitou, and follow the signs
which direct you to the far side of the hill.

🚩 16K 🖂 Philopáppos Hill ☎ 324-4395 🕙 19 May–Sep
Tue–Sat 9:30, Sun 8:15 🖐 Expensive 🚇 Akrópoli 🚌 15

IRÓDIO (ODEON OF HERODES ATTICUS)

This splendid theatre on the southern slopes
of the Acropolis was built in AD161–174 by Tiberius
Claudius Atticus Herodes, a wealthy businessman
from Marathon, in memory of his wife Rigilla.
As well as being the Roman Consul here,

Atticus Herodes was a great patron of the arts, who erected many public buildings in Athens. A good view of the theatre, which seats 5,000, can be had from within the Acropolis itself, though the Odeon is only normally open during the Athens Festival, when it makes a dramatic setting for the drama and music on stage. When first built the theatre had a wooden roof, white marble seating and a mosaic floor. It was restored after World War II, and has been used by the Athens Festival since 1955. It is known locally as the Herodeion.

✝ 17J ✉ Dionysiou Areopagitou ⏰ Open for Athens Festival and other occasional performances 🚇 Akrópoli 🚌 230

MOUSEÍO KOSMÍMATOS ILÍA LALAOÚNI (ILIAS LALAOUNIS JEWELLERY MUSEUM)

Ilias Lalaounis is one of the most famous of modern Athenian jewellers and goldsmiths, and a look around this museum, purpose-built in his old workshop, will explain why. This versatile artist and

craftsman takes inspiration from many sources: Mycenean, Minoan, Byzantine, Viking, Persian and Celtic art, science and more. There are over 3,000 pieces on permanent display, beautifully lit and well captioned in Greek, English and French. A small theatre shows a choice of six short films on his techniques and particular collections, again in all three languages. There are also some delightful works based on designs submitted by children: giant bees and spiders, huge ants and locusts, spaceships, comets colliding, serpents and signs of the zodiac. The museum has a roof garden with views of the Acropolis, a café/restaurant and a well-stocked shop.

➕ 18J ✉ Kallisperi 12 ☎ 922-1044 🕐 Mon, Thu–Sat 9–4, Wed 9–9, Sun 11–4. Closed public hols 👣 Moderate 🍴 Café/restaurant (€€) 🚇 Akrópoli 🚌 230

NAÓS TOU OLYMPÍO DIÓS (TEMPLE OF OLYMPIAN ZEUS)

Known locally as Stíles Olympíou Díos, in its day this was the largest temple in Greece, its day being from about ad 130 onwards, when Emperor Hadrian completed work on it. He dedicated it to Olympian Zeus during the Panhellenic festival in AD132. It was begun in the 6th century BC, with several unsuccessful attempts made to complete the massive project – the temple dwarfed the Parthenon and the Temple of Apollo at Delphi. The 15 columns that remain give a sense of the scale: there were originally 104 of them, each 17m (55ft) high. One crashed spectacularly in 1852 and has been left where it fell. The columns look very impressive at sunrise, and when floodlit.

🚌 19J ✉ Olgas 1 ☎ 922-6330 🕐 Daily 8–7:30. Closed public hols ♿ Expensive. Combined ticket to this and 5 other sites 🚇 Akrópoli 🚌 024, 230

NÉO MOUSEÍO AKRÓPOLIS (NEW ACROPOLIS MUSEUM)

At the time of writing, work was in hand moving the contents of the old Acropolis Museum, on top of the Acropolis, to this gleaming new showcase at the foot of the hill. It was an astonishing operation, involving a series of cranes which carefully transferred the often huge items between each other and then down to their new home, which stands next to the new Acropolis Metro station at the junction of Makriyianni and Areopagitou streets.

The museum's exterior is an impressive sight, with its angular modern design, and the whole building cost €130 million to construct. From the upper windows of a glass gallery you can see the graceful Parthenon, and the hope among many Athenians is that one day the Parthenon Friezes, currently in the British Museum and known there as the Elgin Marbles, will be returned here to their home, where people will be able to see them alongside the building they were designed to decorate. Right at the bottom of the building you can look through the glass floors to see the remains of the old city of Athens that were uncovered during the building of this impressive new museum.

➕ 18J ✉ Makriyianni/Areopagitou ☎ 321-0219 🕔 Phone to check
🔽 Phone to check 🚇 Akrópoli

PANATHINAIKÓ STÁDIO (PANATHENIAN STADIUM)

Best places to see, pages 48–49.

PNÝKAS (PNÝX)

This green and hilly retreat is across the road from the Acropolis, yet few tourists take in this fascinating part of the city. Most visitors are ferried to the Acropolis in coaches and do not have the time, or inclination, to head in the opposite direction. The Pnýx itself is where, in the golden days of Periclean Athens, the Assembly would meet in the 18,000-seat amphitheatre (now

filled with seating for *son et lumière)*, and crowds would gather to hear the great orators of the day.

To the left of the main path, as you walk up beyond the entrance signs, a side path leads to the so-called 'Prison of Socrates'. Visitors should not get too excited, as these two holes in the wall look more like the entrances to a modern public lavatory and there is no historical evidence whatsoever to suggest that this was the prison where the philosopher Socrates was kept after being arrested for allegedly corrupting Athenian youth with his teachings. He was sentenced to death by drinking hemlock and actually died in the state prison in the Agora.

To the right of the main entrance path to the Pnýx, almost opposite the Prison of Socrates, is a Tourist Pavilion set in the trees. In front of the pavilion is a delightful, small church, Ágios Demetrius Loumbardiaris. This was originally built in 1460 and sympathetically rebuilt in 1955. Behind the church and Tourist Pavilion is the Pnýx itself, though access is limited because of its use for the *son et lumière* shows. Further on is the Hill of the Nymphs, also fenced off at the top because it houses an observatory.

✝ 15J 🍴 Cafés (€€) 🚇 Akrópoli 🚌 15

PRÓTO NEKROTAFÍO ATHINÓN (FIRST CEMETERY OF ATHENS)

The First Cemetery is not called that because it is the oldest, but because it is the most important. Here distinguished citizens have a right to be buried, but there is room for more ordinary monuments too. Look for a moving carving of an old man and his wife, her arm resting gently on his – an affectionate portrait of a long-married couple.

One of the graves most interesting to visitors is that of the archaeologist Heinrich Schliemann (1822–1890). It can be found on a small mound beyond the chapel, which is to the left as you enter. Schliemann's tomb was designed by his architect friend Ernst Ziller, who also designed the Presidential Mansion, Olympic Stadium, Schliemann's House and other distinguished buildings in Athens. Also in the First Cemetery is the tomb of Theodoros Kolokotronis (1770–1843), the guerrilla leader hero of the Greek War of Independence against the rule of the Ottoman Empire, and prominent modern citizens, such as the actress/politician Melina Mercouri.

✚ 21K ✉ Anapafseos ⏰ Daily 7–7 ✋ Free 🚌 4

PÝLI ADRIANOÚ (HADRIAN'S ARCH)

Along with the Acropolis and the adjacent Temple of Olympian Zeus, Hadrian's Arch is one of the first ancient sights visitors see when reaching the city centre from the airport. It tells you that you are in a very old city – literally so, as the inscription on one side reads 'This is Athens, the ancient city of Theseus', and on the other, 'This is the city of Hadrian and not of Theseus'. On the Acropolis side of the Arch you were in the ancient city, and on the other side you were in the modern Roman version. Hadrian's marble arch was built in the 2nd century AD, roughly contemporaneous with the Temple of Olympian Zeus.

✚ 19J ✉ Amalias Ⓜ Akropoli 🚌 024, 230

a walk around Mets, Makriyianni and Koukaki

From the Acropolis metro take the exit marked Makriyianni/Areopagos towards the Acropolis.

At the end of the street turn left for the New Acropolis Museum (entrance on your left; ➤ 80) and further, on your right, is the entrance to the Acropolis itself (➤ 38–39).

If you don't want to visit the Acropolis or the new museum yet, turn right at the top of Makriyianni instead of left, and at the end of the street turn left on the busy main road, Amalias.

On your right is Hadrian's Arch (➤ 82–83).

Carry on along Amalias till you see traffic lights and a pedestrian crossing on your right. Cross here and walk back a little way along the other side of the road if you want a closer look at Hadrian's Arch.

Behind you, when looking at the Arch, is the site of the Temple of Olympian Zeus (➤ 79).

Walk back alongside the fence to reach the entrance to the site, on Vasilissis Olgas.

As you leave the Temple site, just to the left of the entrance is a pedestrian crossing, to take you across Vasilissis Olgas to the National Gardens. Cross over here but before going into the Gardens, turn right and walk up to the corner to look at the Panathenian Stadium (➤ 48–49).

Cross over the road if you want to visit, otherwise

*retrace your steps and go into the National Gardens
(➤ 142).*

There is no one particular path to follow, but just walk
ahead to enjoy a stroll through the gardens.

*If you head roughly northwest you will emerge at the
main gates, where you can turn right to walk up to
Syntagma Square, the heart of modern Athens. If
you walk north you will come out on Vasilissis Sofias,
behind the Parliament Building, so turn left to walk
down to Syntagma.*

Distance 3km (2 miles)
Time 2–3 hours with stops
Start point Akrópoli metro ✚ 18J
End point Syntagma metro ✚ 8F
Lunch/tea T Palace (€€; ➤ 157)

THÉATRO DIONÝSOU (THEATRE OF DIONYSUS)

Standing below the Acropolis on its southern slopes, this theatre in its prime held 17,000 people in 64 tiers and was the venue for an annual drama festival. Here, the citizens of Athens witnessed the birth of European drama, in the first theatre ever to be built of stone, where the premieres of plays by Aristophanes, Sophocles and other great dramatists were performed. Initially the theatre was a wooden structure, followed by a stone building in 342–26BC, and finally by the Roman theatre whose remains are what can be seen today. There are some amusingly detailed Dionysian statues supporting the stage, and marble barriers from the times when wild animals fought in the arena, which was also used for gladiatorial contests. In the front rows are the marble thrones for visiting dignitaries. In the rock behind the theatre is a cave which was once held sacred to the Goddess Artemis, and where a Byzantine chapel was later built.

🚩 18J ✉ Entrance to southern slopes of Acropolis on Dionysiou Areopagitou ☎ 322-4625 🕐 Daily 8–7:30 (closes 5pm Nov–Mar). Closed public hols 👣 Expensive. Combined ticket to this and 5 other sites 🚇 Akrópoli 🚌 230

HOTELS

Acropolis View (€)

You don't have to pay a fortune to get a view of the Acropolis, as this simple but clean and well-run little hotel can offer just that from many of its rooms, as well as from its rooftop terrace. The 32 rooms are basic and on the small side, but all have private baths, TVs, air-conditioning and mini-fridges.

✉ Webster 10 ☎ 921-7303 www.acropolisview.gr 🚇 Akrópoli

Athenian Caillirhoe (€€)

This 5-star designer hotel is not as expensive as its rating suggests. It has 81 rooms, 3 junior suites, sound-proofing, air-conditioning and some rooms with views of the Acropolis. There's also a bar, restaurant and roof garden on the 8th floor during the summer months, with views of the Acropolis, a free gym and sauna, and a business centre for guests.

✉ Kallirois 32 ☎ 921 53 53 www.tac.gr 🚇 Syngrou-Fix

Hera Hotel (€€)

The stylish Hera combines 21st-century chic with a classical look in the public rooms. The six deluxe rooms on the 6th floor all have balconies and excellent views of the Acropolis, as does the rooftop Peacock restaurant, which opens in the summer months, while downstairs there's a bar.

✉ Falirou 9 ☎ 923-6682 www.herahotel.gr 🚇 Akrópoli

Herodion Hotel (€€)

The 4-star Herodion Hotel is right by the New Acropolis Museum, and not far from the Acropolis metro station. It has its own bar, coffee shop and restaurant, as well as a roof terrace where you can indulge yourself in one of the two jacuzzis while enjoying views of the Acropolis.

✉ Rovertou Galli 4 ☎ 923-6832 www.herodion.gr 🚇 Akrópoli

Marble House Pension (€)

Just a short walk from the southern side of the Acropolis is this quiet, friendly and inexpensive little hotel. Half the rooms are en suite, some have vine-covered balconies, all are clean, and the owners are extremely helpful.

✉ Zinni 35a, Koukaki ☎ 923-4058; www.marblehouse.gr 🚇 Syngrou-Fix

Philippos Hotel (€€)

This is a good mid-range choice for the Makriyanni district, with its own restaurant, bar and coffee shop. All rooms have phones, TVs, air-conditioning and private bathrooms.

✉ Mitseon 3 ☎ 922-3611; www.philipposhotel.gr 🚇 Akrópoli/Syngrou-Fix

RESTAURANTS

Edodi (€€€)

One of the most renowned restaurants in the city, Edodi offers modern cuisine with exciting food combinations and an ever-changing menu. The interior manages to be both stylish and modern, yet with homely touches such as wooden dressers and old mirrors. Booking is absolutely essential.

✉ Veikou 80 ☎ 921-3013; www.edodi.gr 🕐 Mon–Sat 7–midnight. Closed Aug 🚇 Syngrou-Fix

Karavitis (€)

In winter the dining room is cosy with wine barrels all around, and in summer they open a courtyard dining area across the street, bringing a touch of Greek village life to the streets of Athens.

✉ Arktinou 33–35 ☎ 721-5155 🕐 Nightly 7pm–late 🚇 Evangelismos

Mets (€€)

If you want a relaxed evening in this neighbourhood head for the old favourite, Mets, a combination of jazz bar and casual restaurant where the food, the wine and the music are reliably good.

✉ Markou Moussourou 14 ☎ 922-9454 🕐 Daily noon–2am 🚌 209

Spondi (€€€)

It's worth booking a meal at this French-influenced establishment, one of only a handful of Athens restaurants to win – and keep – the coveted Michelin star, hidden away in an impressive 19th-century town house behind the Panathenian Stadium (➤ 48–49).

Whether you go for the simple fresh sea bass or more complex creations, it's likely to be one of your best meals in Athens.
✉ Pyronnos 5 ☎ 752-0658; www.spondi.gr ⏰ Mon–Sat 8pm–1am
🚌 2, 4, 11

Strofi (€)
With great views of the Acropolis from the roof, Strofi is understandably popular, serving good Greek taverna staple dishes such as stifado, moussaka and grills.
✉ Rovertou Galli 25 ☎ 921-4130 ⏰ Mon–Sat dinner 🚌 230

Vyrinis (€)
This long-established family taverna, with its popular courtyard garden, is behind the Panathenian Stadium (► 48–49) and so way off the tourist track. There's a good selection of starters, so this may be the place to go Greek and have several plates of *meze*.
✉ Arhimidous 11 ☎ 701-2021 ⏰ Mon–Sat lunch and dinner 🚌 2, 4, 11

SHOPPING

Korres
The first homeopathic pharmacy in Athens opened here behind the Panathenian Stadium (► 48–49) and has spread to stores all over the world. You can buy healthy treats like pomegranate cream, basil lemon shower gel and absinthe shaving cream for men.
✉ Eratosthenous 8 ☎ 756-0600; www.korres.com

Ilias Lalaounis Museum Shop
It could be dangerous to visit the Ilias Lalaounis Museum (► 78) because you're sure to want to buy one of his exquisite creations in the wonderful museum shop. There is also a bookshop with a good range of publications on arts and crafts.
✉ Kallisperi 12 ☎ 922-1044

Stoa
Opposite one of the entrances to the Acropolis metro station is this collection of arts and crafts shops, named after the ancient Greek style of colonnade where such shops could be found. Here

you will find contemporary ceramics, paintings, jewellery and other lovely items of the kind that make great gifts.

✉ Makriyianni 5

ENTERTAINMENT

BARS AND CLUBS
De Luxe
De Luxe has a downstairs bar that gets noisier as the night goes on, and an upstairs restaurant which is quieter, but just as much fun and serves good food until 1:30am. The bar stays open later.

✉ Falirou 15 ☎ 924-3184 🕐 Daily 9pm–late, kitchen open till 1:30am
🚇 Akrópoli

Lambda Club
One of the most popular gay clubs in Athens, the Lambda has been around for years, but remains as busy as ever, and has drag shows on some nights.

✉ Lembesi 15 ☎ 942-4202 🕐 Nightly, closed Aug 🚇 Akrópoli

JAZZ
Douzeni
After a meal in one of Makriyianni's excellent eating places, move on to some late-night singing and *bouzouki* music.

✉ Makriyianni 8 ☎ 922-7597 🕐 Closed Sun

Half Note
Live jazz is on offer most nights from international bands in this well-established venue in the Mets district (west of the Stadion). The club opens at 10, but beware the hefty admission fee.

✉ Trivonianou 17 ☎ 923-2460 or 921-3310 🕐 Closed Tue, summer

SOUND AND LIGHT
A superb sight at any time, the Acropolis is illuminated and on show from the theatre on Filopáppou Hill, clearly marked from the entrance opposite the southern slopes of the Acropolis.

☎ 322-5904 🕐 1 Apr–31 Oct. English nightly 9; German, Tue, Thu 10; French 10 all other nights

The Acropolis and the Plaka

Visiting the Acropolis is the one thing that almost every visitor to Athens does on their first time in the city, and often on subsequent visits too, such is the draw of one of the world's most beautiful and fascinating buildings: the Parthenon.

Walk down the northern side of the hill and you find yourself in the old town of Athens, the Plaka, unless you take a right turn and get lost in the maze of streets that make up the little village-like district of Anafiotika.

While the Plaka is very touristy, it still also has a character of its own, with some lovely old mansions, small museums, back-street tavernas and a lively nightlife. It's also the area where you'll find other ancient remains, including the Roman Agora, the Ancient Agora, the Tower of the Winds and Hadrian's Library.

AÉRIDES (TOWER OF THE WINDS)

This, the best feature in the Roman Agorá site (➤ 101), can be seen easily from outside the fencing, but you should take a closer look. The curious octagonal building dates from about 40BC. One of its many features was a water clock, driven by a stream from the Acropolis; it still has its weather vane, compass and sundials, and a frieze depicting the eight wind gods. One of these, Ailos, gives his name to Eolou Street, on which the tower stands.

➕ 17H ✉ Pelopidha/Eolou ☎ 324-5220 ⏰ Daily 8–7:30 (closes 5pm Nov–Mar). Closed public hols ✋ Expensive. Combined entrance ticket to this and 5 other sites 🚇 Monastiraki

ÁGIOI APÓSTOLI (CHURCH OF THE HOLY APOSTLES)

The site of one of the oldest churches in Athens is inside the Agorá excavations and, though these are impressive enough, no visitor should miss looking inside this lovely church. It dates from AD 1000–1025, but was much changed over the centuries. It was restored to its original form in 1954–56. The church was built above the ruins of a Roman nymphaeon (sanctuary of nymphs) from the 2nd century AD. The frescoes in the narthex (porch) are post-Byzantine and were moved here when the neighbouring church of Ágios Spyridon was demolished. The wall paintings in the church itself were found beneath the modern plaster.

➕ 16H ✉ Inside the Agorá ☎ 321-0185 ⏰ Tue–Sun 8–7:30, Mon 11–7:30 (closes 5pm Nov–Mar). Closed public hols ✋ Expensive. Combined ticket to this and 5 other sites 🚇 Thissio/Monastiraki

AGORÁ

Best places to see, pages 36–37.

AKRÓPOLI (ACROPOLIS)

Best places to see, pages 38–39.

ANAFIÓTIKA

Finding this lovely area of Athens is like stumbling unexpectedly upon a Greek island village. In fact, location apart, that is just what it is. When King Otto wanted a palace built for himself after assuming the Greek throne in 1832, he was told that the best builders in Greece came from the Cycladic island of Anafi, to the east of Thíra (Santorini). Once summoned, the builders knew they would be away for several years, and so they re-created their island home, complete with white cube houses and donkey-wide paths, at the foot of the Acropolis. The best way to approach the Acropolis is through Anafiótika, where home-made signs point the way and prevent you wandering into someone's garden by mistake.

✚ 17H 🚌 230

ÁREIOS PÁGOS (AREOPAGOS)

Almost opposite the Acropolis entrance, some stone steps carved in the rock next to a plaque lead up to the Areopagos. This is where the supreme court of Athens once stood. The name means the Hill of Mars, and the legend is that here Mars (Ares to the Greeks), the God of War, was tried for murdering one of the sons of Poseidon. It is also where Orestes stood accused of murdering his mother, Clytemnaestra, in the Aeschylus play *Eumenides*. It was from the Areopagos that St Paul delivered his sermon to the Athenians in AD54, and the text is inscribed on the plaque near the steps. The site has open access and is more noted for its views than for its few ancient remains.

✚ 16J 🕐 Open access 🖐 Free 🚇 Monastiraki/Thissio or Akrópoli

ELLINIKÓ PAITHÍKO MOUSEÍO (HELLENIC CHILDREN'S MUSEUM)

This is an enjoyable venture, although small and a little improvised. Its maze of rooms includes work rooms, play rooms and displays on such subjects as the building of the new Athens metro lines. This allows children to don hard hats and wield shovels as they learn about the ongoing metro construction sites. Other fun activities include the ancient (dressing up in old clothes) to the modern (a computer). Contact the museum for current details. Although some of the staff speak English and other languages, and welcome all children, advance notice for visits by non-Greek-speaking children is advisable.

🚉 19H ✉ Kydathinaíon 14 ☎ 331-2995; www.hcm.gr 🕐 Tue–Fri 10–2, Sat–Sun 10–3. Closed Jul–Aug 🖐 Free 🚇 Syntagma

EVREIKÓ MOUSEÍO TIS ELLÁTHOS (JEWISH MUSEUM OF GREECE)

The exhibits in this fascinating museum on the edge of the Plaka are displayed on nine levels radiating around an octagonal atrium. The ground floor contains, among other things, the restored interior of a 1920s synagogue, moved here from Patra. Themed exhibits include the ancient biblical origins of the arrival of Judaism in Greece in about the 2nd century BC, a celebration of Jewish culture and its colourful costumes and the dreadful years of the Holocaust, which completely wiped out many Greek Jewish communities, such as those in Kastoria, Crete and Drama. Only larger communities, such as those in Athens and Thessaloniki, survived, and then only barely. A gift shop on the ground floor sells souvenirs, postcards, replicas of exhibits and a good selection of books covering Jewish history in Greece.

🚉 19H ✉ Nikis 39 ☎ 322-5582; www.jewishmuseum.gr 🕐 Mon–Fri 9–2:30, Sun 10–2. Closed Sat, Greek and Jewish public hols 🖐 Moderate 🚇 Syntagma

MNIMEÍO LYSIKRÁTOUS (MONUMENT OF LYSICRATES)

This unassuming marble monument, in a small square off the main Plaka streets, has a fascinating history. It was built in 334BC and is the city's only complete surviving choregeic monument. These were built as tributes to the winners in an annual music and drama festival at the nearby Theatre of Dionysus (➤ 86). Lysikrates was the sponsor *(choregoi)* behind the winning team, as an inscription around the monument explains. The team was the chorus in a drama competition the previous year, and the monument originally included the tripod, which victors were traditionally awarded. There were once many such monuments around here, hence the name of the street, Tripodou. In more recent times, the six-columned building was converted by monks into a library, and it was while in the library in 1810 that Lord Byron wrote some of his epic poem, *Childe Harold's Pilgrimage*.

✚ 18J ✉ Plateía Lysikrátous
Ⓐ Akropoli

MOUSEÍO ELLINIKÍS LAIKÍS TÉCHNIS (MUSEUM OF GREEK FOLK ART)

Greece preserves its folk traditions well, both in everyday life and in museums such as this one, in the Plaka district. On the ground floor are embroidery displays from the different island groups and also from the mainland. Ali Pasha's court at Ioannina exerted a strong influence on local embroidery, importing rich fabrics from the Near East and from as far away as Iran and Uzbekistan.

The Mezzanine displays some ornate spinning wheels, shuttles and spindles, together with examples of work, such as a pillowcase woven by nomadic Sarakatsan shepherds. There are some bread seals, for both family and religious occasions (though frequently in Greece, the one is the other), including one that imprints on the loaf 'The one who eats of my body and drinks of my blood'. There are also several masquerade costumes, the most famous of which is probably the Skyros Goat Dancer, the Yeros, with his masked face, sheepskin coat and dangling bells. A permanent display on the same floor is dedicated to the folk artist Theofilos Hatzimichael (c1868–1934). Especially worth seeing is the Theofilos room, dating from 1924–30, from a house on Lesvos, where every inch of wall space is covered in primitive but vibrant paintings, including Alexander the Great, folk hero Katsantonis and political hero Kolokotronis.

✚ 19H ✉ Kydathinaíon 17 ☎ 322-9031 🕐 Tue–Sun 9–2. Closed public hols 🖐 Moderate 🚇 Syntagma

MOUSEÍO ELLINIKÍS PAITHIKÍS TÉCHNIS (MUSEUM OF GREEK CHILDREN'S ART)

This smart little museum, devoted to displaying and encouraging the artistic work of Greek children, is a delightful idea, and overseas visitors with children will be equally welcomed. The museum began as a private collection of Greek children's art, which was originally on display in the Milies Museum on the Pilion peninsula, but was brought to Athens and expanded. There are some enchanting displays of paintings, small sculptures and puppets, all showing the original and vivid imagination which can only come from a child. The main paintings are inspired by annual competitions on themes such as Greece and the Sea, Mother and Child, designing a Greek stamp or telling a Greek folk tale, with the winning paintings all being for sale. If you cannot afford an original, many of them have been turned into notes and postcards for sale in the small shop.

The gallery is upstairs, while downstairs are bright, lively rooms, with painting and drawing equipment and puzzles, where regular activity sessions are held. If you don't speak Greek but would like to visit or would like your child to join in, then a phone call in advance will ensure that an English-speaking helper is on hand.

www.childrensartmuseum.gr

✚ 19H ✉ Kodrou 9 ☎ 331-2621 ⏱ Tue–Sat 10–2, Sun 11–2. Closed public hols and Aug 🖐 Inexpensive; children and students free 🚇 Syntagma 🚌 024, 230

MOUSEÍO ELLINIKÓN MOUSIKÓN ORGÁNON (MUSEUM OF GREEK MUSICAL INSTRUMENTS)

The mansion was built in 1842, and outside is a courtyard which hosts occasional concerts in the summer. Off the courtyard is the shop, with an extensive collection of recordings and books on Greek music. The interior of the mansion has three floors devoted to the subject of Greek musical instruments. This is only part of the collection of over 1,200 instruments, dating back to the 18th century, amassed by musicologist Fivos Anoyanakis.

Inside the entrance is a small video display area showing films covering the making and playing of different instruments. The fun starts with the display cases themselves, however, as most of them have headphones attached, enabling you to listen to the instruments being played. A brief introduction in Greek, then English, tells you which instrument you are listening to, the name of the tune and where it was recorded. The instruments are grouped according to type and many are exquisite works of craftsmanship. Take a look at some of the lyres and guitars, in particular. On a simpler level, one set of photographs shows you how to make music using worry beads and a wine glass! There are also rural instruments such as bagpipes and shepherd's pipes, and examples of the urban blues known as *rembetika*.

➕ 17H ✉ Diogenous 1–3 ☎ 325-0198/4119 🕐 Tue, Thu–Sun 10–2, Wed 12–6. Closed Mon and public hols ✋ Free 🚇 Monastiraki

MOUSEÍO KANELLOPOÚLOU (KANELLOPOULOS MUSEUM)

This neoclassical mansion in the Plaka is easily visited while walking up to the Acropolis, and merits a lengthy look. The house itself was built in 1884 and has been renovated to show off the private collection, put together over the years by Paul and Alexandra Kanellopoulos and now owned by the Greek government. The collection is very well displayed on several floors, with information available in Greek and English, although more details about specific objects rather than general descriptions of the contents of each case would be welcome.

As with any private collection it is eclectic, and this one ranges from the sacred to the profane. The latter is represented by erotic carvings of satyrs chasing, and sometimes catching, nymphs around the typical Greek red-on-black vases, which were being

made in Athens in the 7th century BC. The sacred is represented by an extensive collection of icons on the ground floor. There is also some Mycenean gold and examples of arts and crafts by the Minoans and Phoenicians and from Egypt, Italy and elsewhere. The collection ranges from the 3rd century BC to the 19th century. The huge block of stone on the ground floor fell from the Acropolis. There is intricate Persian jewellery, and bead and glass work. Statues are also a feature, as is a fine bust of Alexander the Great.

✚ 17H ✉ Panos/Theorias
☎ 321-2313 ⏰ Tue–Sun, 8:30–3. Closed public hols
✋ Inexpensive
Ⓜ Monastiraki

NAÓS IFÉSTOU (TEMPLE OF HEPHAISTOS)

This fine temple dominates the western side of the Agorá
(➤ 36–37). It is also known as the Thiseío (Theseion) – as is the
surrounding area of Athens – because some of its friezes show
Theseus, one of the mythical Kings of Athens and son of Aegeus,

after whom the Aegean Sea is named. Hephaistos was god of fire and art as well as god of metallurgy and, just as the potters' quarter was at nearby Keramikós (► 115), so this was the blacksmiths' and metalworkers' area. The temple was built in about 449–444BC, and the start of its construction launched the Golden Age of Pericles (► 38). It is easily the best-preserved building in the Agorá, if not one of the best in all of Greece.

✚ 16H ✉ In the Agorá, Adrianou 24 ☎ 321-0185 ⏰ Tue–Sun 8–7:30, Mon 11–7:30 (closes 5pm Nov–Mar). Closed public hols ✋ Expensive. Combined ticket to this and 5 other sites 🚇 Thissio/Monastiraki

ROMAIKÍ AGORÁ (ROMAN AGORA)

This is one of the few archaeological sites in Athens that is scarcely worth the price of admission. Its chief feature is the Tower of the Winds (► 92), which can, in any case, easily be seen from outside the walls. Apart from this, the mainly ground-level ruins are somewhat diminished by weeds and the packs of cats and dogs which have taken up residence. The small, attractive Fethiye Mosque, built in 1458 and dedicated by Sultan Mehmet II, is nowadays surrounded by lovely orange trees, but only used as a storeroom. Opposite the site entrance are the remains of a Medresse, an Islamic seminary which was destroyed by Greeks rebelling against the Turks during the War of Independence. It had

been a prison and the tree in the courtyard was used for hangings.

✚ 17H ✉ Pelopidha/Eolou ☎ 324-5220 ⏰ Daily 8–7:30 (closes 5pm Nov–Mar). Closed public hols ✋ Expensive. Combined entrance ticket to this and 5 other sites 🚇 Monastiraki

a walk around the Byzantine churches of Athens

Starting in Mitrópoli Square, walk up the street left of the main cathedral.

On your right is the 16th-century chapel of Ágia Dynamis.

Go up to the bottom corner of Syntagma Square and turn right along Filellinon. The tower of the Church of St Nikodimos is visible.

To visit this Byzantine church, cross over the busy road. Further along is the Church of St Paul.

Cross back over Filellinon and look for the Museum of Greek Folk Art sign. Follow this down Kydathinaíon.

On your right is the 12th-century Byzantine church dedicated to the Transfiguration of Jesus Christ.

Further down Kydathinaíon is a small square surrounded by cafés. Cross this diagonally to the far right corner and walk down the short street.

Reach the 11th-century Church of St Catherine.

Past the church, turn right up Adrianou, then first left, climbing to the T-junction. Turn right.

This is Anafiótika (➤ 93), the area below the Acropolis.

Follow the narrow street and the signs for the Acropolis, past the Church of St George on the Rocks and the 1774 Church of St Simeon.

This brings you to the site of the first university of the independent Greek state. It is now a small museum.

Turn right after the university down Klepsithras to the Roman Agora. Skirt right then left around the Agorá, right down Eolou and right again up pedestrianized Ermou.

Ahead is the Kapnikaréa (➤ 112), yet another of the many ancient churches that survive in the centre of Athens.

Pass Kapnikaréa and take the first right to return to Mitrópoli Square.

Distance 2.5km (1.5 miles)
Time 1 hour without stops, 2–3 hours with stops
Start/end point Mitrópoli Square ✚ 18G
🚇 Monastiráki
Tea Kapnikarea Café (€) ✉ Christofolou 2
☎ 322-7394

HOTELS

Acropolis House (€)

This inexpensive, family-run Plaka option is in a restored 19th-century mansion on a quiet, traffic-free street. It is well maintained, though not all rooms have a private bath.

✉ Kodrou 6–8 ☎ 322-2344; www.acropolishouse.gr Ⓜ Syntagma

Adonis (€)

The Adonis is a good, standard, economic hotel with helpful staff, conveniently located in a pedestrian street right at the edge of the Pláka and not far from Syntagma Square. It has a breakfast room/bar with Acropolis views and attracts many regular visitors.

✉ Kodrou 3 ☎ 324-9737 Ⓜ Syntagma

Adrian Hotel (€€)

You can't be closer to the centre of Plaka life than an address on Adrianou, and this hotel also has a roof garden which looks up to the Acropolis rock. Some rooms have lovely balconies. The rates are reasonable, particularly in winter.

✉ Adrianou 74 ☎ 322-1553; www.douros-hotels.com Ⓜ Monastiraki

Central Hotel (€€)

The Central is a really good mid-range choice in the heart of the city, close to the Syntagma metro yet right on the edge of the Plaka. It's very modern and stylish without being over-expensive. There's a restaurant just off the striking atrium, and the rooms have modern facilities, including internet access.

✉ Apollonos 21 ☎ 323-4357; www.centralhotel.gr Ⓜ Syntagma

Electra Palace (€€€)

The Electra Palace is a real luxury option at the heart of the Plaka, with a rooftop pool and views of the Acropolis. Facilities include an indoor pool, gym, sauna and steam bath, plus a restaurant on the rooftop in summer. All rooms have air-conditioning, TV, telephone and mini-bar. It's within walking distance of Syntagma Square and most of the main sights.

✉ Nikodimou 18 ☎ 337-0000; www.electrahotels.gr Ⓜ Syntagma

Imperial (€€)

Despite the name and location, close to Syntagma Square and overlooking Mitrópoli, this is a moderately priced hotel with a friendly staff and clean rooms. It's also within walking distance of most of the main sights.

✉ Mitropoleos 40 ☎ 322-7617 🚇 Monastiraki

Kouros (€)

The Kouros, formerly a mansion, is ideally placed in a quiet street with several small hotels, close to the heart of the Plaka. It offers no frills, but the rooms are clean.

✉ Kodrou 11 ☎ 322-7431 🚌 Airport bus

Magna Grecia (€–€€)

This 4-star boutique-style hotel is a member of the Great Small Hotels of the World group, in a late 19th-century house designed by Ernest Schiller, right by the cathedral. There are ten stylish rooms, all with TV, DVD, CD players and wireless internet access. Rates are surprisingly cheap for the quality on offer.

✉ Mitropoleos 54 ☎ 324-0314 www.magnagreciahotel.com 🚇 Monastiraki

Metropolis Hotel (€)

The delightful Metropolis, a pink-coloured building half-covered in bougainvillaea, is an inexpensive and friendly hotel, where the rooms are basic but perfectly comfortable, and a bargain for a location right in the heart of Athens. Not all have private bathrooms, so check first.

✉ Mitropoleos 46 ☎ 321-7469 www.hotelmetropolis.gr 🚇 Monastiraki

Nefeli (€€)

This is a small, family-run hotel of just 18 rooms. With many regular visitors, it is inexpensive, friendly, modern, spotlessly clean and convenient for both the Plaka and the city centre.

✉ Yperidou 16 ☎ 322-8044 🚇 Syntagma

RESTAURANTS

Bakalarakia (€)

Here you'll find simple but good Greek food in what claims to be the oldest taverna in Athens, established in 1865. Salted cod in garlic is the speciality, which gives this basement place its name.

✉ Kydathinaíon 41 ☎ 322-5084 🕒 Mon–Sat 7–12. Closed midsummer 🚇 Monastiraki

Daphne's (€€€)

Daphne's is popular with visiting celebrities, but you don't have to be a movie star or politician to enjoy the superb contemporary takes on traditional Greek food. The *stifado* here is exceptional. There's a lovely quiet courtyard for the summer evenings, and a good list of regional Greek wines.

✉ Lysikratous 4 ☎ 322-7971 🕒 Daily 7pm–1am 🚇 Akrópoli

The Five Brothers (€–€€)

This friendly spot has an ideal location, under some shady trees near the Tower of the Winds. The waiters are relaxed and the food superior to that in some other tavernas in the area. Try the Vine-Grower's Lamb or Beautiful Ellen's Veal.

B Eolou 3 ☎ 325-0088 🕒 Daily 8am–1am 🚇 Monastiraki

Glykis (£)

This little neighbourhood restaurant is in the Plaka but slightly off the main tourist drag, so attracts the locals who like the cheap prices and good home-cooked food.

✉ Angelou Geronta 2 ☎ 322-3925 🕒 Daily 10am–late 🚇 Syntagma

Klimataria (€)

A simple taverna in the upper part of the Plaka that's been here for over a hundred years – so it must have been doing something right. The food is simple but tasty meat and fish dishes, and often there's live music thrown in for good measure.

✉ Klepsidras 5 ☎ 321-1215 🕒 Nightly 7pm–late 🚇 Monastiraki

Ouzeri Kouklis/Sholarhio (€€)

This wonderful place is packed out every lunchtime and night. Waiters bring a tray of the day's dishes to your table; you pick what you want, and pay a fixed price, a bargain, with drinks included.

✉ Tripodon 14 ☎ 324-7605 www.sholarhio.gr ④ Daily 11am–2am
Ⓜ Akrópoli

I Palia Taverna tou Psara (€€–€€€)

This famous fish restaurant also offers plenty of exceptional meat dishes. Try the plate of appetisers and a glass of ouzo while you make your choice

✉ Erechtheos 16 ☎ 321-8733 ④ Daily 10am–1am Ⓜ Monastiraki

Platanos (€)

Dining under the plane tree that gives Platanos its name is a tradition that seems to have been around for as long as Athens itself. In winter diners retreat to the cosy indoors but in summer the courtyard opposite the restaurant fills with diners tucking into hearty Greek favourites like tender roast lamb or juicy *stifado*.

✉ Diogenous 4 ☎ 322-0666 ④ Mon–Sat 12–4:30, 8–12 Ⓜ Monastiraki

I Saita (€)

This unpretentious basement taverna offers wine from the barrel and a standard menu that occasionally features some delicious surprises, such as pork in a cream of celery sauce.

✉ Kydathinaíon 21 ④ Daily dinner ▣ 024, 230

To Ypogeio tis Plakas (€)

A great basement place, with murals by local artist George Savakis. It has good, simple Greek food such as *souvlaki* and *calamaris*, and retsina straight from the barrel.

✉ Kydathinaíon 10 ☎ 322-4304 ④ Daily 7pm–2am

Xinos (€€)

In a Plaka back street, this is very popular with Athenians, offering superior food, music and a lovely outdoor garden.

✉ Angelou Geronta 4 ☎ 322-1065 ④ Daily 8pm–midnight. Closed in winter

SHOPPING

ANTIQUES, ARTS AND CRAFTS

To Anoyi

The owner of this studio specializes in her own painted icons and eggs, but also sells the work of other Greek artists: ceramics, sculptures, blankets and wall-hangings.

✉ Sotiros 1 ☎ 322-6487

Archipelagos

Among the souvenir shops in the Plaka are places selling fine work, like this one with a good selection of jewellery and ceramics.

✉ Adrianou 142 ☎ 323-1321

L'Atelier

Here you'll find good copies of Greek antiquities, such as vases, frescoes and Cycladic statues.

✉ Adrianou 116 ☎ 323-3740

The Athens Gallery

This stylish gallery represents the work of a handful of contemporary Greek artists. It's expensive but exquisite.

✉ Pandrossou 14 ☎ 324-6942

Byzantino

Byzantino sells its own hand-made jewellery, gold pendants, rings, brooches and other beautiful items.

✉ Adrianou 120 ☎ 324-6605

Gallerie Areta

A small offshoot of the Athens Gallery, the Areta contains mainly ceramics and paintings, including some good primitive artwork.

✉ Pandrossou 31 ☎ 324-3397/894-0217

Karamikos Mazarakis

As well as traditional Greek *flokati* rugs and *kilims*, this shop sells wool and silk rugs from the rest of the world.

✉ Voulis 31–33 ☎ 322-4932

Kostas Sokaras

This shop sells an intriguing mix of embroidery, jewellery, Greek folk costumes and traditional shadow theatre puppets.

✉ Adrianou 25 ☎ 321-6826

Olive Wood Workshop

This crafts outlet in a Plaka side street selling beautiful olive-wood carvings, including bread boards, cheese boards and bowls, most of which are made by the owner.

✉ Mnisikleous 8 ☎ 321-6145

Pyromania

There are some tasteful examples of handblown glass, ceramics and olive-wood carvings, with a small workshop at the rear where the artist-owner may be at work.

✉ Kodrou 14 ☎ 325-5288

Tasos Sandal and Leather Store

Leather is always a good buy in Greece and here in the Plaka there are several stores which produce and sell their own leatherware, including belts, sandals, wallets and handbags.

✉ Adrianou 83 ☎ 322-4150

BOOKS, NEWSPAPERS AND MAGAZINES

Compendium

This is the place to find English-language books, magazines, guides, fiction, books about Greece, maps and a large second-hand section for exchanging your used paperbacks. There's also a notice-board for language courses, apartments to rent etc.

✉ Nikis 25 ☎ 322-1248

FOOD AND DRINK

Brettos

This well-stocked drinks shop in the Plaka district specialises in own-brand spirits and liqueurs as well as a wide range of Greek drinks such as ouzo and Metaxa.

✉ Kydathinaíon 41 ☎ 323-2110

Mesogaia

This store on the edge of the Pláka specializes in products from all over Greece, including the best Kalamata olives and olive oil, honeys, preserves, cheeses, tea, ouzo, raki and other treats.
✉ Nikis 52 ☎ 322-9146

ENTERTAINMENT

BAR
Brettos

A Pláka institution, Brettos sells liquor by day, but turns into a bar at night where the liquor is sold in glasses rather than bottles.
✉ Kydathinaion 41 ☎ 323-2110

TAVERNAS AND CLUBS WITH MUSIC
Palia Taverna Kritikou

Popular with tour groups, this taverna has Cretan music and traditional dancing.
✉ Mnissikleous 24 ☎ 322-2809

Perivoli t'Ouranou

If you want some genuine Greek *rembetika* blues music, the long-established Perivoli is the place to head for dinner and a live show, though it does close for the summer.
✉ Lysikratous 19 ☎ 323-5517

Stamatopoulou Palia Plakiotiki Taverna

Locals and visitors enjoy the authentic Greek music, though the only dancing is done by the customers.
✉ Lysiou 26 ☎ 322-8722

Taverna Mnissikleous

On offer here are late-night music and dancing shows, every night of the week till the early hours. It often caters for tour groups.
✉ Mnissikleous 22 ☎ 322-5558

Monastiraki, Psyrri and Gazi

This has undoubtedly been the most exciting area in Athens for several years now. At one time most visitors would scarcely venture out of the Plaka, and there would certainly be little reason to visit Psyrri and Gazi.

MONASTIRAKÍ

But Psyrri has had a startling make-over, and where old workshops and warehouses once stood, you now find *ouzeries*, restaurants, music clubs and art galleries. Attractions like the superb Benáki Museum of Islamic Art have also helped revitalize this quarter of Athens. The neighbouring district of Gazi hasn't quite been transformed to the same extent yet, but it's heading that way, with the addition of the Technopolis arts centre on the borders of Gazi and Psyrri. Monastiraki also has been given a little smartening, with a brand new Metro station and pedestrian walkways.

ATHINAÍS

It's something of a trek to get out to Athinais, and you should check what's happening there before you go, as this arts centre has changing programmes and exhibitions in its various areas – museum, gallery, cinema, theatre and music hall – not to mention exhibition spaces, two restaurants and a bar. The building dates from the 1920s, when it was constructed as a silk factory, but this closed down in the 1950s and it was used as a storage facility and not much else till it was transformed into this exciting project at the turn of the 21st century.

One permanent display here is at the Pierides Museum of Ancient Cypriot Art, which has several galleries housing a small but very select collection covering 9,000 years of the Cypriot civilization. The ceramics are especially impressive, and when it opened in 2001 this was the first museum in Greece to be devoted to the culture of Cyprus.

🔡 1E 🖂 Kastorias 34–36 ☎ 348 0000; www.athinais.com.gr 🕐 Daily 9:30am–10pm, but individual exhibitions and events may vary. Cypriot Art Museum daily 9:30–7 💷 Moderate for exhibitions 🍴 Two restaurants and a bar (€€) 🚌 813

KAPNIKARÉA

In 1834, when Ermou Street was built, there was talk of destroying this delightful Byzantine church, which stands right in the middle of the long, straight road opposite the Parliament Building. Thankfully Ludwig of Bavaria, father of Otto, the first King of the Greeks, intervened, and the church was saved. The present building dates back to the 13th century, though there was a church here as long ago as the 11th century. Since 1931 it has belonged to the University of Athens, who helped to restore it. Inside, the walls are lined with paintings, though they can be hard to distinguish unless it's very sunny.

🔡 6F 🖂 Ermou/Kapnikareas ☎ 322-4462 🚇 Monastiraki

KÉNTRO ELLINIKÍS PARÁDOSIS (CENTRE OF HELLENIC TRADITION)

Up some stairs in an arcade between Mitropoleos and Pandrossou is this excellent outlet for Greek artists and craftsmen working in traditional styles. Here you can find furniture, jewellery, ceramics, hand-painted signs, paintings, embroidery and all manner of ideas for good-quality souvenirs. On the second floor are temporary arts and crafts exhibitions, and another display area where more expensive antiques are for sale. On the first floor is also a very good café and restaurant.

🟥 17G ⊠ Pandrossou 36/Mitropoleos 59 ☎ 321-3023 (café) 🕐 Daily 9–8 (closes 7pm in winter) 🚻 Free 🍴 Café (€) 🚇 Monastiraki

KERAMIKÍ SYLLOGÍ MOUSEÍOU ELLINÍKIS LAIKÍS TÉCHNIS (CERAMIC COLLECTION OF THE MUSEUM OF GREEK FOLK ART)

The mosque in which this collection is housed was built in 1759 on the site of a fountain. Since the state of Greece was founded it has been a barracks for the army band, and then a hospital. It specializes in ceramics from Greece and Cyprus from the first half of the 20th century. The 794-piece collection is part of that of Professor Vassilios Kyriazopoulos, who built it up over 50 years.

One fascinating aspect of the museum is that it tells the stories, in Greek and English, of some of the potters whose work is on display. Minas Avramides, for example, was an uneducated stonemason before becoming a potter in Thessaloniki, where his son still operates a workshop. His drawings of men, gods and beasts are primitive, but the finished plates have a colourful boldness. Avramides also designed a Greek alphabet using animal motifs. Nikolaos Yasiranis (1901–73) was from Rhodes, his father having been a clay modeller in Asia Minor, from where many of the craftsmen featured originated. The son's clay models depicting characters from folk traditions are delightful and amusing, showing a wicked eye for human nature. In the gallery upstairs are small themed collections from outside Greece, from Macedonia, Thessaly and from the islands. The colourful decorated plates from Rhodes, with their bold reds, blues and greens, are a typical example. The white, bright interior of the mosque's dome has been restored, but patches of the original, faded, painted brickwork still show through.

🔲 17G ✉ Tzami Tsistarakis, Areos 1 ☎ 324-2066 🕐 Wed–Mon 9–2:30. Closed public hols ♿ Inexpensive Ⓜ Monastiraki

KERAMIKÓS (KERAMIKOS CEMETERY)

This principal cemetery of ancient Athens was in the Keramikos, or potters' quarter of the city. Keramos was the patron saint of potters: hence, ceramics. The cemetery contains tombs and archaeological finds dating back to the 12th century BC, when it was first used for burial purposes. Many tombstones have been

replaced as they were, lining the grand Street of the Tombs, which was reserved for the rich. One such, the Tomb of Dionysios of Kollytos, a wealthy Athenian treasurer, is marked by a fine statue of a powerful bull. Others range from the ostentatious to the simple but powerfully moving.

There is also abundant wildlife here, attracted by the stream that flows rather sluggishly through the grounds. Tiny terrapins can be seen in the grass, in the trees are chaffinches and black redstarts, and olive trees and other plants grow in profusion. It can be a peaceful haven from the traffic of the city, except on Sunday mornings when the noisy flea market takes place outside the walls.

The museum here is named after Gustav Oberlander, an industrialist who provided funds towards the excavation of the site in the 1930s. It contains good displays of the potter's art, as well as examples of *ostraka*, or voting tablets for Athenian elections, from which the term ostracism is derived. There are also some incredibly poignant gravestones, such as the one containing this message from a grieving father: 'This monument, Xenophantes, your father created for you on your death, Sophilos, for whom you, in parting, created sorrow'.

✚ 3F ✉ Ermou 148 ☎ 346-3552 🕐 Tue–Sun 8–7:30, Mon 11–7:30 (daily 8–5 Nov–Mar). Combined ticket for this and 5 other sites available 💰 Expensive 🚇 Thissio

MITRÓPOLI (ATHENS CATHEDRAL)

Two very contrasting churches stand side by side in Mitrópolis Square. The smaller is the Mikrí Mitrópoli (Little Mitrópolis), a 12th-century church dedicated to Ágios Eleftherios. It has a haunting cave-like atmosphere: do go in if you find it open. It is dwarfed by its huge neighbour, the Megáli Mitrópoli (Great Mitrópolis), the Cathedral of Athens, a modern building on the site of a monastery that stood in the square until 1827. The cathedral's main exterior feature is its fine entrance. Above this is a mosaic of the Annunciation (*Evangelismos*), which gives the church its official name.

✠ 18G ✉ Plateía Mitropoleos ✋ Free Ⓜ Monastiraki

MOUSEÍO ISLAMIKÍS TÉCHNIS (MUSEUM OF ISLAMIC ART)

The fine art collection amassed by the cotton merchant Emmanuel Benáki was so vast that much of it remained in storage when only the main Benáki Museum (▶ 44–45) was open, even though that was spread over several floors. When that main museum was refurbished the opportunity was taken to open some annexes to display more of the items, and this collection in Psyrri, which brings together the art works that Benáki collected from the Islamic world, is quite stunning.

It isn't just the quantity of Benáki's collection that is impressive, it is the quality of individual items. He was definitely a man who had an eye for only the finest objects. Here they are, beautifully displayed over four floors in roughly chronological order. A map in each room shows the extent of the Islamic world in the period being covered, and the items are labelled with some detail in both Greek and English. The rooms are spacious and the light is low, adding a certain drama to many of the best items.

Room 1 includes a collection of metalwork from Egypt and Iran from the 7th to 12th centuries, and illuminated Egyptian manuscripts from the 10th to 14th centuries. Room 2 contains some wonderfully vivid turquoise ceramics, whose colours look as bright as the day they were fired, while Room 3 includes a fascinating display of astronomical instruments and Room 4 has some jewel-encrusted rifles and other arms among its breathtaking objects. Don't miss the views from the roof terrace either, even if you don't want to enjoy a snack in the café.

✚ 4E ✉ Asomaton 22 ☎ 325-1311; www.benaki.gr ⏰ Tue, Thu–Sun 9–3, Wed 9–9. Closed Mon and public hols ✋ Moderate 🍴 Café (€) 🚇 Monastiraki

PINAKOTHÍKI DÍMOU ATHINÉON (CITY OF ATHENS ART GALLERY)

Walk down the busy main street of Pireos from Omonia Square and on your left you reach this under-rated modern Greek art collection, well worth knowing about if the National Gallery is closed. The gallery's building dates from 1872, when it was the Foundling Hospital, and the collection itself has been acquired since 1923. It covers a wide range of 19th- and 20th-century subjects, including evocative old street scenes and archetypal Greek landscapes, showing how the face of Greece has changed over the years. There are portraits of proud peasants, and examples of Greece's tradition of primitive artists. The extensive collection of engravings includes works by the great masters of this art and their followers and works by young engravers.

✚ 4E ✉ Pireos 51 ☎ 324-3022 ⏰ Mon–Fri 9–1, 5–9, Sun 9–1. Closed Sat and public hols ✋ Free 🚇 Omonia

PLATEÍA MONASTIRAKÍOU

Best places to see, pages 50–51.

TECHNOPOLIS

In 1857 work started on building a gasworks in Athens, which opened in 1862 and gave its name to this area of the city: Gazi. Most people reach it by walking past the Keramikos Cemetery, which gets its own name because it was the part of ancient Athens where the ceramic workers all lived. Trades and buildings come and go, but the names often remain.

In 1984 the gasworks closed, but some of the buildings and the equipment have been retained and transformed into this startling cultural centre that has helped to regenerate this once run-down industrial part of Athens since it opened in 1999. The complex is worth seeing for its own sake, even when no special exhibition is on, as its industrial sculptures and buildings can still be enjoyed. But it is best appreciated when there is an art or photography exhibition on, or by attending one of the evening concerts that range from dance to music, rock to classical.

One permanent attraction here is the Maria Callas Museum, dedicated to the singer who was born in New York but returned to Athens with her Greek mother at the age of 13. It was in Greece that she received her musical education and her startling talent first showed itself. The museum (open Mon–Fri 10–3, free) is only a tiny collection of personal items but interesting if you're there when it's open.

✚ 13H ✉ Pireos 100 ☎ 46-0981 🕐 Mon–Fri 9–9 during exhibitions ✋ Free 🚇 Thissio

VIVLIOTHÍKI ADRIANOÚ (HADRIAN'S LIBRARY)

This group of buildings, near the Agorá, was built by Emperor Hadrian some time after AD132 to house his library, but the building design incorporated a walled courtyard around a central garden and pool. This may sound modest, and today's ruins might suggest that was the case, but it was an extensive building – the largest that Hadrian built in Athens – and the courtyard contained 100 columns. The library has been re-opened to the public after a long period of excavations, but there is not a great deal to see and not much information available within the site at the time of writing.

✚ 17H ✉ Eolou 🕐 Daily 8–3 ✋ Free 🚇 Monastiraki

a walk around Psyrri and Gazi

At the northwest corner of Plateía Monastirakíou walk west along the far side of the busy main street, Ermou.

This is the point where the pedestrianized Ermou of designer shops and international chain stores gives way to the traffic-filled Ermou of workshops and junk shops.

Cross directly over the little square with a church in the middle to find that Ermou is again pedestrianized and leads to the Keramikos Cemetery on your right.

If time allows, visit the Keramikos Cemetery and its small museum (➤ 115). Facing you past the cemetery at the end of Ermou is Technopolis (➤ 118–119).

Cross the street to see if anything is on at Technopolis, then cross back again to continue the walk, turning left up Pireos. Turn right down Asomaton to the Museum of Islamic Art Museum, on the left.

You should definitely visit this off-shoot of the main Benáki Museum (➤ 44–45), as it brings together under one roof the finest items from the Islamic world (➤ 116–117).

On leaving the museum turn left to continue along to the end of Asomaton. Turn left on Sarri, and right on Anargyron, one of the main streets of Psyrri. Turn right down Miaouli to arrive back at the Metro station and square at Monastiraki.

Distance 2.5km (1.5 miles)
Time 1 hour without stops, 2–3 hours with stops
Start/end point Plateía Monastirakíou ✚ 17G 🚇 Monastiraki
Lunch Sigalas (€; ➤ 124))

HOTELS

Attalos (€€)

Simple, but clean and well-equipped, Attalos offers friendly service and is very convenient for Psyrri, the Plaka, the flea market and Monastiraki metro if you are heading for the ferries or the airport.

✉ Athinas 29 ☎ 321-2801 Ⓜ Monastiraki

Carolina (€)

The Carolina is a refurbished budget establishment. Some rooms are en suite and most are small, but they are clean and the hotel is a convenient central base for exploring the sights of the city.

✉ Kolokotroni 55 ☎ 324-0944 Ⓜ Monastiraki

Erechthion (€)

The Erechthion is a very basic 2-star hotel with 22 rooms, and its price and location make it very popular with budget travellers. The rooms are definitely frill-free, but they do have TVs and air-conditioning, and are kept clean.

✉ Flammarion 8 ☎ 345-9606 Ⓜ Thissio

Eridanos (€€)

This chic and sleek 5-star designer hotel near the Keramikos Cemetery is right in the heart of the 'new' Athens of Psyrri and Gazi. It has one luxury rooftop suite, seven rooms with views of the Acropolis, seven more with balconies and most rooms have hydro-massage facilities. All have internet access, direct phones, satellite TV and mini-bar with complimentary soft drinks.

✉ Pireos 80 ☎ 520-5360; www.eridanus.gr Ⓜ Monastiraki

Jason Inn (€)

This 3-star hotel has 57 guest rooms and is functional and friendly rather than being fancy. It is right in the heart of Monastiraki, but the rooms do have sound-proofing, and its rooftop restaurant/bar (open in summer) has terrific views of the Acropolis. A good, safe, inexpensive choice.

✉ Asomoton 12 ☎ 325-1106; www.douros-hotels.com Ⓜ Thissio

Ochre & Brown (€€)

The Ochre & Brown is one of the best of the string of boutique hotels that have transformed the Athens accommodation scene in the last few years. There are just 10 rooms and many items that other hotels charge as extra come free here: wifi, breakfast and newspaper, for example. This is European-style elegance in the heart of Psyrri.

✉ Leokoriou 7 ☎ 331-2950; www.ochreandbrown.com Ⓜ Thissio

Omega Hotel (€)

This basic option is in the Psyrri district, between Monastiraki and the Central Market. Rooms have been renovated and they all have private bathrooms, phones and TV; some have air-conditioning, mini-fridges and views of the Acropolis. The lack of air-conditioning can be a major problem in summer, so check before booking.

✉ Aristogonos 15 ☎ 321-2421; www.omega-hotel.com Ⓜ Monastiraki

Tempi (€€)

Very central, this small, clean budget place is popular with students and others who prefer a friendly atmosphere to frills, though half of the 24 rooms do have private showers and a few have views of the Acropolis – just!

✉ Eolou 29 ☎ 321-3175; www.tempihotel.gr Ⓜ Monastiraki

RESTAURANTS

AristeraDexia (€€€)

Another of the new names that has brought some pizzazz to the Gazi district, with its open kitchen, glass ceiling on the wine cellar, and 21st-century versions of traditional Greek dishes.

✉ Andronkou 3 ☎ 342-2380 🕔 Mon–Sat 9pm–1am Ⓜ Thissio

Hermion (€€)

This long-established café-restaurant is just off the flea market. It has indoor seating, an attractive courtyard dining area and good-quality, moderately priced Greek favourites.

✉ Pandrossou 7–15 ☎ 324-6725 🕔 Daily breakfast, lunch, dinner
Ⓜ Monastiraki

Mamacas (€€)

This post-modernist taverna in a 1920s barrel house in Gazi serves good traditional Greek menu and fashionable with the Athens arts set.

✉ Persefonis 41, Gazi ☎ 346-4984 ⏰ Daily lunch and dinner. Closed Aug Ⓜ Thissio

Pil Poul (€€€)

For the best of modern Greek cooking try this Michelin-starred place, whose dishes reflect the whole Mediterranean, with Middle Eastern dashes. Also a rooftop terrace with views of the Acropolis.

✉ Apostolou Pavlou/ Poulopoulou ☎ 342-3665 ⏰ Mon–Sat lunch and dinner Ⓜ Thissio

Sigalas (€)

The bustle of Monastiráki and its flea market seems to spill inside this century-old taverna. It's always busy, and it's cheap, with a wide range of Greek dishes, and frantic but good service.

✉ Plateía Monastiraki 2 ☎ 321-3036 ⏰ Daily 7am–2am Ⓜ Monastiraki

Symposio (€€€)

Symposio combines superior food with a relaxed atmosphere and a very popular late-night bar in an elegant house. The menu blends international and Greek dishes, such as pasta with cheese from Metsovo.

✉ Erechthiou 46 ☎ 922-5321 ⏰ Mon–Sat dinner 🚌 230

Taverna tou Psyrri (€)

One of the eating places that has transformed this district. The taverna's owner is from Naxos, which is reflected in his menu: good imported fish, meat and other produce.

✉ Aischylou 12 ☎ 321-4923 ⏰ Daily 10am–2am Ⓜ Monastiraki

Varoulko (€€€)

This is still primarily a fish restaurant, and as fish is never cheap anywhere, be prepared for a big bill, but also for some of the best sea bass and monkfish that you will ever eat. The summer rooftop dining gazing out at the Acropolis makes this a very special occasion.

✉ Pireos 80 ☎ 522-8400; www.varoulko.gr 🕔 Daily 8pm–late ▣ Thissio

Vitrina (€€€)

This chic eatery in Psyrri is setting the standards for both decor and food: lamb with mushrooms and red peppers in a sweet and sour port sauce is a regular dish.

✉ Navarchou Apostoli 7 ☎ 321-1200 🕔 Tue–Sat dinner, Sun lunch
🚇 Monastiraki

SHOPPING

ANTIQUES, ARTS AND CRAFTS

Iakovos Antiques

On offer are ceramics, paintings and knick-knacks, not just from Greece but from around the world.

✉ Ifestou 6 ☎ 321-0169

Melissinos Art

The family business of the famous poet-sandalmaker Stavros Melissinos has relocated from the Plaka to the Psyrri district, but the hand-made sandals remain the same quality as before. Stavros's son maintains the tradition, which has seen the sandals worn by celebrities including Peter O'Toole and John Lennon.

✉ Ayias Theklas 2 ☎ 321 9247; www.melissinos-poet.gr

Motakis

This sprawling junk/antique shop in a sizeable basement is typical of the Monastiraki market. Established for almost a century, it sells everything from exquisite antiques to offbeat curios.

✉ Plateía Abyssinia 3 ☎ 321-9005

Nasiotis

Look for the display of old photos, engravings, books, magazines and saucy postcards in this Aladdin's cave. Beneath is a cavernous jumble of books.

✉ Ifestou 24 ☎ 321-2369

ENTERTAINMENT

ARTS CENTRE
Bios
A multimedia arts centre offering music, drama and art shows.
There's also a café with DJs and videos playing.
✉ Pireos 84 ☎ 342-5335; www.bios.gr ⏲ Daily 11am–4am 🚇 Thissio

BARS
Apsenti
The Thession area gets plenty of visitors by day, to the shops and
the flea market, but in the evening the feel changes as the cafés,
restaurants and bars draw a different clientele. Apsenti has a good
drinks menu and is a great place to relax late at night.
✉ Iraklidon 10 ☎ 346-7206 ⏲ Daily 10am–late

Astron
Loud yet laid-back, the Astron is one of the most popular bars in
Psyrri, and also one of the smallest.
✉ Taki 3 ☎ 6937-146337 or 0977-469356 (mobiles) ⏲ Daily 9:30pm–4am

Inoteka
Popular bar in the flea market area of Monastiraki, which only
really gets going late in the evening.
✉ Plateía Abyssinia 3 ☎ 324-6446 ⏲ Daily 1pm–late
🚇 Thissio/Monastiraki

MUSIC VENUES
House of Art
The House of Art concert venue has been around forever, since
long before Psyrri became fashionable, putting on shows that
range from Greek music legends to touring international stars to
jazz, blues, poetry and plays.
✉ Sahtouri 4 ☎ 321-7678 ⏲ Closed summer

Stavlos
An arts complex with exhibitions, occasional movies and live jazz.
✉ Iraklidon 10 ☎ 346-7206; www.stavlos.gr

Omonia and Exarchia

If you come to Athens for ancient monuments and pretty views of the Acropolis, then this part of the city will definitely disappoint. It is not the most attractive area, but it does have an earthy authenticity about it, a bustle and clamour of the kind that is slowly disappearing from the quarters that have been modernised and pedestrianised recently.

EXÁRCHIA

Most people come to the area at some point, as it is where you find the National Archaeological Museum, one of the finest museums in the world, which along with the Acropolis is an essential part of every Athens visit. What most people won't see is a site of modern historical significance; the Athens Polytechnic building played a major part in the overthrow of the Colonels' Regime. Further south, Omonia Square exemplifies Athens today: prettified but still gritty.

EPIGRAPHIKÓ MOUSEÍO (EPIGRAPHICAL MUSEUM)

Housed in the same building as the National Archaeological Museum, but with the entrance around the corner in Tositsa Street, the Epigraphical Museum is a specialist collection that contains over 13,000 different Greek inscriptions. It may lack the wider appeal of the archaeological collection, but for the historian or other interested visitor, it is fascinating and it is the most important collection of its kind in the world. The stone inscriptions contain all manner of historical records, such as the official decree from Themistocles which ordered Athens to be evacuated prior to the expected Persian invasion in 480BC. One of the oldest in the collection dates back to 510BC, and the mostly Greek inscriptions run through till the early Christian era. There are financial records for the building of the Parthenon, tax records, voting records, information about the supply of water to Athens and many more absorbing items, from the nationally important to the personal and mundane – which is what history is.

✉ 6B ✉ Tositsa 1 ☎ 821-7637 ⏰ Tue–Sun 8:30–3
✋ Free 🚇 Omonia

ETHNIKÓ ARCHEOLOGIKÓ MOUSEÍO (NATIONAL ARCHAEOLOGICAL MUSEUM)

Best places to see, pages 40–41.

ETHNIKÓ ISTORIKÓ MOUSEÍO (NATIONAL HISTORICAL MUSEUM)

This archive of historical documents and artefacts is displayed in the former Greek Parliament building, built in 1858 and home to the Parliament until 1934. One of the chief attractions is the grand Debating Hall of the Old

Parliament. The museum is likely to be mainly of interest to historians, while admirers of Lord Byron will find a room containing some of his belongings, such as his sword, desk, trunk, pistol and helmet. The rooms tell the story of modern Greek history, from about the 14th century until shortly after independence. There's a large collection of weaponry, and tributes to the freedom fighters who helped Greece gain independence. It is very Greek centred, with numerous paintings of Greek worthies. Unfortunately, only summarised information is available in anything other than Greek (English and French).

🚹 7E 📧 Stadiou 13 ☎ 323-7617 ⏱ Tue–Sun 9–2. Closed public hols
♿ Moderate 🚇 Syntagma

KENTRIKÍ AGORÁ (CENTRAL MARKET)

To the south of Omonia, where Athinas meets Evripidou, is the 19th-century metal structure that houses the city's main meat and fish markets. This bustles with business six days a week, and inside you will find every type of fish from the Aegean and beyond, and every cut of every meat you're likely to find on a Greek plate. It is not a place for vegetarians to linger. Instead, they may wish to explore the streets which radiate from here, where other markets and fascinating shops can be found, displaying fruit, vegetables, flowers, nuts, spices, olives, cheese and much more. On a sunny day, photographers can be seen taking shot after shot of the rainbow-coloured displays. It is definitely the place to visit to see

Athenians bartering, and to buy something tasty to take home. It is also the place to go if you're planning a picnic for a day out.

➕ 6E ✉ Athinas/Evripidou ⏰ Mon–Sat early to late 🍴 Several near by (€) 🚇 Omonia

MOUSEÍO TIS PÓLEOS ATHINÓN (CITY OF ATHENS MUSEUM)

Despite being the original Royal Palace, home of King Otto between 1836 and 1842, this is an easily missed small white building on the south side of Plateía Klafthmonos. The refurbished royal apartments are surprisingly modest, and the walls display many prints and paintings of Athens over the years, including work by the British artists Edward Lear and J M W Turner. Also on display is King Otto's copy of the 1843 Greek Constitution, and there are changing exhibitions in the ground floor galleries.

www.athenscitymuseum.gr

➕ 7E ✉ Paparigopoulou 7 ☎ 324-6164 ⏰ Mon, Wed–Fri, 9–4, Sat–Sun 10–3. Closed Tue and public hols 🎫 Moderate 🚇 Panepistimio 🚌 1, 2, 4, 5, 11, 12

PLATEÍA EXARCHÍON (EXARCHIA SQUARE)

There isn't a lot to see in Exarchia Square, a tiny neighbourhood square, but it's at the centre of life in this rather special if run-down part of the city, Exarcheia. It's very lively at night (the best time to visit) and at lunchtime too, when the handful of bars, cafés and restaurants around the square fill with local people – but very few tourists. The area has plenty of students, as the Polytechnic (▶ 133) is just down the road, and it also attracts artists, writers and intellectuals. The square may lack charm and beauty, but it certainly has character.

➕ 7B

PLATEÍA KLAFTHMÓNOS (KLAFTHMONOS SQUARE)

This square off Stadiou literally means the Square of Wailing. Traditionally, civil servants from the many surrounding ministries come here to complain after being dismissed. At the bottom end stands the Byzantine Church of Ágioi Theodoroi (St Theodore), which was built in the 11th century and is one of the contenders for the oldest church in Athens. This is also the square where you will find the National Historical Museum (► 128–129).

🚼 7E 🖂 Off Stadiou 🚇 Panepistimio

PLATEÍA OMONÍAS (OMONIA SQUARE)

Omonia (Harmony Square) is the second most important square in Athens after Syntagma, or Constitution Square. For many years this has been rather an ironic name, as Omonia has long been just about the least harmonious part of the city. It was – and still is – a busy traffic hub, with seven major streets converging here and people using the Metro station adding to the crowds. A few blocks up is the National Archaeological Museum, and a few blocks down is the Central Market, which also add to the congestion.

Omonia has been spruced up a little in recent years, with the opening of the new Metro station and some rather smart hotels nearby, though there's a long way to go before the square is as pleasant to be in as Syntagma now is. It's still one of the poorer parts of the city, and attracts many immigrants who hang round looking for work, or trying to sell cheap goods on the streets. It is now undeniably more pleasant than it was ten years ago, but it still attracts a certain number of people who you might not want to be hanging around with late at night.

🚼 6C 🚇 Omonia

POLYTECHNÍO (POLYTECHNIC)

In April 1967, a military coup in Greece ushered in a dictatorship as the country became ruled by 'The Junta', a right-wing regime of army colonels. The Colonels' Regime was greeted with horror by many in the land that gave birth to democracy in Europe. The regime was sworn in as the official government by the ousted King Constantine, an act that he later claimed was forced upon him but it served to link him forever with the hated colonels in the eyes of most Greeks.

Instead of a royal rebellion against the military dictatorship, it was the ordinary young students of Athens who played a prime role in ousting the Junta. In November 1973 they occupied the Polytechnic building in protest against the government who were increasingly repressing freedom. It came to a head on 17 November 1973 when a tank broke down the gates of the Polytechnic and shots were fired, killing an unknown number of students. It was not quite the end of the Junta, but it precipitated it. In 1974 there was a failed military coup in Cyprus, which resulted in the Turkish invasion of Northern Cyprus, and it was this, on top of the killing of its own young citizens, that eventually brought about the downfall of the military regime. The killings of 17 November are still commemorated on that date. Anyone visiting the National Archaeological Museum should walk a block south to see where those momentous modern events happened.

✚ 6B ✉ Patission 42 Ⓜ Omonia

a walk around urban Athens

From the southern end of Omonia Square walk down Athinas on the left-hand side of the road. A few blocks down you cross the bottom of the newly improved Kotzia Square.

On your right as you pass across the bottom of Kotzia Square is the Town Hall. The elegant building at the far side of the square on your left is the headquarters of a bank.

Continue on down Athinas and you pass, on your left, the Central Market. Beyond the market turn left on Evripodou till you reach Eolou. Turn left on Eolou, which takes you back across the top of Kotzia Square. Cross carefully over two very busy main roads, and the street becomes Patission, also called 28 October Street. Stay on the right-hand side of the road.

Patission takes you, after several blocks, to the National Archaeological Museum on your right.

After visiting the Museum (➤ 40–41) turn left back down Patission and turn left again along Stournari.

Along here, on your left, are the buildings of the Polytechnic (➤ 133), scene of the student protests of November 1973.

At the end of Stournari is Exarchia Square (➤ 131). Walk to your right around the square and look for Themistokleous at the far right corner. Take this street all the way down, crossing the main street of Akadimias, after which you each another main street, Venizelou. Turn right here to return to Omonia Square.

Distance 2km (1.2 miles)
Time 1 hour with stops
Start/end point Omonia Square ✚ 6C
🚇 Omonia
Lunch Meat Me (€€; ➤ 138)

HOTELS

The Alassia (€€)

The Alassia is a good choice for single travellers as 24 of its 82 rooms are singles, and all have air-conditioning, sound-proofing, internet, mini-bar, music, direct-dial phone and satellite TV. It's located just behind Omonia Square, a convenient and comfortable choice for this part of town.

✉ Sokratous 50 ☎ 527 4000 www.thealassia.com.gr 🚇 Omonia

Baby Grand (€€)

The Baby Grand is one of the best of the new breed of fun, boutique hotels in Athens. Many of its rooms have been dubbed 'graffiti' rooms, as they have been designed by comic book and other artists. The Spiderman room is a great favourite, and the hotel's spa facilities, Moet & Chandon Champagne Bar and Meat Me restaurant make it a top choice.

✉ Athinas 65 ☎ 325-0900 www.classicalhotels.com 🚇 Omonia

Delphi Art Hotel (€€)

Just a few blocks west of Omonia is this delightful 1930s mansion which has been converted into a smart boutique-style hotel with 36 rooms and 4 suites. The rooms are stylishly decorated and have high-speed internet, satellite TV and music facilities; some have jacuzzis too.

✉ Ayiou Konstandinou 27 ☎ 524-4004; www.delphiarthotel.com 🚇 Omonia

Exarchion (€)

This inexpensive hotel is close to the National Archaeological Museum (➤ 40–41) in the lively student area of Exarchia. All rooms are *en suite* with air-conditioning, and many have a balcony.

✉ Themistokleous 55 ☎ 380-1256 🚇 Omonia

Grand O' Hotel (€€€)

The 5-star Grand O' has been revamped, with many of its 115 rooms and suites handed over to some of Athens' finest designers to come up with their own room schemes. Though the official room rates are high, there are often internet bargains, and the location – close to Omonia Metro station – is ideal for this part of the city.

✉ Pireos 2 ☎ 523-5230; www.classicalhotels.com

Museum (€€)

Behind the National Archaeological Museum, but overlooking its gardens, this quiet and well-maintained Best Western hotel is a good affordable option if you want to be in this area. All rooms are en suite and have air-conditioning, sound-proofing, high-speed internet and telephone.

✉ Bouboulinas 16 ☎ 380-5611; www.hotelsofathens.com 🚇 Omonia

Orion (€)

The Orion is very cheap, but is a perfectly acceptable place if you're on a strict budget. Located in the lively Exarchia district, it is great for student nightlife but a long walk from the Omonia metro. Compensations include a pleasant rooftop terrace for breakfast and lots of authentic local eating places close by.

✉ Emmanuel Benaki 105 ☎ 382-7362 🚇 Omonia

Titania (€€€)

This huge hotel with high standards is handily placed for both Omonia and Syntagma squares, and only a short walk from the Plaka and the National Archaeological Museum. It offers well-equipped rooms with cable TV and high-speed internet access, room service, a restaurant and a roof bar with views of the Acropolis. A bonus for drivers is parking space for 400 cars.

✉ Panepistimiou 52 ☎ 330-0111 🚇 Omonia/Panepistimio

RESTAURANTS

Barba Yannis (€)

This great favourite in a student area frequently has queues outside the door. There is impromptu music (not always), brisk service, and a limited menu of good Greek dishes is on offer. You won't find a better atmosphere.

✉ Emmanuel Benaki 94 ☎ 330-0185 🕐 Daily lunch and dinner. Closed Aug 🚇 Omonia

Costoyannis (€€)

This great taverna has a good reputation for appetisers and fish dishes, and a better-than-average house wine.

✉ Zaimi 37 ☎ 821-2496 🕓 Mon–Sat dinner 🚇 Omonia

Ideal (€€€)

The Ideal is elegant and slightly expensive, but with attentive service and an extensive and interesting menu, including 'drunkard's titbits' (pork in tomato sauce with olives, onions, mushrooms and cheese) or prawns with feta.

✉ Panepestimiou 46 ☎ 330-3000 🕓 Mon–Sat noon–midnight 🚇 Omonia

Meat Me (€€)

On the ground floor of the Baby Grand Hotel is this Athens offshoot of a successful Thessaloniki restaurant, which serves top-quality taverna-style food at reasonable prices in a chic setting.

✉ Baby Grand Hotel, Athinas 65 ☎ 325-0900 🚇 Omonia

Melrose (€€)

No city is complete without its Pacific Rim restaurant, and this is Athens's finest. Seafood, naturally, is good – salmon, shrimps, swordfish – together with stylish decor and superb service.

✉ Zosimadou 16 (off Kallidromiou) ☎ 825-1627 🕓 Mon–Sat dinner. Closed Aug 🚇 Omonia

Taygetos (€)

Taygetos is a cheap and cheerful grill place close to Exarcheia Square and is great if you just want a quick but filling meal.

✉ Satovriandou 4 ☎ 523-5352 🕓 Mon–Sat 9am–1am 🚇 Omonia

SHOPPING

DEPARTMENT STORES

Hondos Centre

The city's best-known department store is right on Omonia, and while it's far from sophisticated, you might well find some bargains here if you can elbow your way through the Greek shoppers.

✉ Plateía Omonia 4 ☎ 528 2800

Notos Galleries
Close to the junction where Eolou meets Stadiou is this collection of over 400 shops in one huge multi-level department store. Very good for high-street woman's fashions and perfumes.
✉ Eolou 99 ☎ 324-5811

Notos Galleries Home
This large branch on several floors of the Notos chain concentrates on home items. The kitchenware section is particularly interesting.
✉ Kotzia Square ☎ 324-5811

FOOD AND DRINK
Asimakopouli
This renowned Athenian patisserie is a must for anyone with an extremely sweet tooth. Greeks like their sweets sweeter than most.
✉ Charilaou Trikoupi 82 ☎ 361-0092

Bachar
Bachar is a specialist shop, near the Central Market, concentrating on a large range of spices and herbs for both culinary and medicinal use.
✉ Evripidou 31 ☎ 321-7225

The Olive Shop
A great varity of olives and other Greek foodstuffs. Situated in the Central Market (➤ 130–131).
✉ Athinas/Evriidou

ENTERTAINMENT
BARS
Bar Guru Bar
Funky bar in the market area where there's live jazz and an impressive drinks list. It's popular with the arty Athenian crowd who frequent it till the early hours.
✉ Plateía Theatrou 10 ☎ 324-6530 www.bargurubar.gr
🕓 Daily 9pm–late

Moet & Chandon Bar

The first champagne bar in Athens, Moet & Chandon is a very relaxing oasis inside the Baby Grand Hotel on the first floor. Superior snacks, fine wines and champagnes, and lovely big easy chairs to chill out in.

✉ Baby Grand Hotel, Athinas 65 ☎ 325-0900 ⏰ Daily 11am–11:30pm

DISCOS/ROCK CLUBS

Ennea Ogdoa

Some *rembetika* nights, but otherwise Greek pop music. Great atmosphere.

✉ Alexandras 40 ☎ 823-5841/882-1095

Frankosyriani

This popular venue In Exarchia is run by a musician.

✉ Arachovis 57 ☎ 380-0693

Stoa Athanaton

Established favourite in the Central Market, with authentic music and good food, but book ahead.

✉ Sofokleous 19 ☎ 321-4362 ⏰ Lunch, evening. Closed Sun

Taximi

Very popular Exarchia folk/*rembetika* club.

✉ Isavron 29 ☎ 363-9919 ⏰ Closed Jul–Aug

THEATRE

Hellenic American Union Auditorium

This offers a wide range of theatre and music shows, all in English and with, naturally, a strong American bias.

✉ Massalias 22 ☎ 362-9886; www.hau.gr

National Theatre of Greece

These are generally Greek-language productions of international dramas, though occasionally a visiting theatre group will perform in their own language.

✉ Agiou Konstantinou 22 ☎ 523-3322; www.n-t.gr

Syntagma and Kolonaki

Syntagma Square – Constitution Square – is the very centre of Athens. It's a rallying point, the seat of Parliament, a place to rendezvous and relax, and a tourist attraction too. It's changed in recent years, and for the better. When the new Metro station was opened, Syntagma once again became a pleasant place to meet and to hang out, the kind of heart that all cities need.

KOLONÁKI

SÝNTAGMA

It's not surprising that Kolonaki, the area alongside Syntagma, became one of the most upmarket parts of Athens. It is where you'll find art galleries, antique shops and designer fashion stores. Just off Syntagma is also where you'll find several of the city's most interesting museums: the Benáki, the Cycladic Art Museum, the War Museum and the Byzantine Museum. And beyond these museums, all more or less in a row, is the National Gallery.

ETHNIKÍ PINAKOTHÍKI (NATIONAL GALLERY)

Like much of the rest of the city, the National Gallery has benefited from the Olympic Games effect, with a major make-over in recent years. Instead of the previous rather jumbled displays there is now a chronological approach to the collection. As the focus is exclusively on Greek art, from ancient to modern times, most visitors do need an explanation of the various periods and artistic movements in Greece, which are far from familiar to outsiders.

The most famous Greek painter of them all, El Greco, is represented by several works, but it helps to see what he grew out of, and how he changed the face of Greek painting. An audio tour is available in Greek or English, and is well worth taking. The displays are on two floors with the upper floor devoted to the 20th century, and there are also galleries where major international exhibitions can be displayed; these are now coming to Athens in greater numbers. Do check out if anything is on during your visit, in case you need to allow more time.

➕ 12D ✉ Vasileos Konstantinou 50 ☎ 723-5937 🕐 Mon, Wed 9–3, 6–9, Thu–Sat 9–3, Sun 10–2. Closed public hols 💶 Expensive 🍴 Café 🚇 Evangelismos 🚌 234

ETHNIKÓS KÍPOS (NATIONAL GARDENS)

Also known as the Royal Gardens, these were created in the 1840s under the direction of Queen Amalia, wife of Otto, the first King of Greece. They cover 16ha (40 acres) and offer a shady, peaceful retreat from the noisy city streets: ponds filled with fish and terrapins, tree-lined paths, fountains, cafés and children's play areas. Other attractions include a children's library and a small Botanical Museum. Less pleasing are stray cats and a sad attempt at a zoo. At the southern end stands the Zappeion, built in the late 19th century by two wealthy Greek-Romanians as an exhibition hall, and now used as a conference centre.

➕ 20G 🕐 Daily sunrise–sunset 💶 Free 🍴 Cafés (€) 🚌 2, 4, 11, 12

LYKAVITÓS (LYCABETTUS HILL)
Best places to see, pages 42–43.

MOUSEÍO BENÁKI (BENÁKI MUSEUM)
Best places to see, pages 44–45.

MOUSEÍO KYKLADIKÍS TÉCHNIS (MUSEUM OF CYCLADIC ART)
Best places to see, pages 46–47.

NOMISMATIKÓ MOUSEÍO ATHINÓN (ATHENS NUMISMATIC MUSEUM)
Not far from Syntagma Square along the
street popularly known as Panepistimio and
officially known as Venizelou, stands the
mansion where the discoverer of Troy,
Mycenae and much else besides once lived.
Designed and built for Heinrich Schliemann by
Ernst Ziller, this grand mansion now houses
the Numismatic Museum, a collection of
some of the six hundred thousand coins
encompassing examples from the Hellenic,
Roman, Byzantine, medieval and modern
eras, along with medals, seals and a hoard
of gems. Digital touch screens and a multimedia room bring the museum into the
21st century.

✚ 8E ✉ Panepistimíou 10–12 ☎ 364-3774
🕐 Tue–Sun 8:30–3 💷 Moderate 🚇 Syntagma
🚌 23, 25, 230

PLATEÍA SYNTÁGMATOS (SYNTAGMA SQUARE)
Best places to see, pages 52–53.

POLEMIKÓ MOUSEÍO (WAR MUSEUM OF GREECE)

Don't be put off by the name or by the military hardware outside this museum, for inside is a fascinating collection covering many aspects of Greek history. As just one example of its all-encompassing brief, it includes copies of some dramatic friezes from the remote Temple of Vassai on the Peloponnese, regarded as one of the most outstanding Greek temples outside Athens. The friezes show military conflict, and art lovers will appreciate stumbling across such skilful replicas of otherwise relatively inaccessible pieces.

The museum covers conflicts dating back to the Greek myths, the Trojan Wars and the tales of Homer. There are first-class models of many of the fortified towns in Greece, such as Náfplio (➤ 172–173) and Mystras, and others showing great battle scenes from Greek history. World War II is covered in some depth, including the Battle of Crete and the sufferings of the Athenian population. There is also an extensive collection of weaponry and uniforms. Outside the museum is a display of military vehicles. Children will enjoy climbing up to peer inside the cockpits of the Spitfires and Tiger Moths, and getting a close look at the anti-aircraft guns and some fairly primitive World War I hardware. Having examined the outside displays, go inside and take the stairs or lift to the top floor, working your way down, though the layout on the several floors is not strictly chronological. This makes more sense of a visit, though, and you may wish to take a break in the café in the basement afterwards.

✚ 11E ✉ Vasilissis Sofias 22/Rizari 2 ☎ 724-4464 🕔 Tue–Sun 9–2. Closed public hols ♿ Free 🍴 Café (€) Ⓜ Evangelismos 🚌 234

PROEDRIKÓ MÉGARO (PRESIDENTIAL MANSION)

The present-day home of the Greek President was once the Royal Palace, until the Greek monarchy was officially abolished after a Referendum in 1974, following the overthrow of the Greek Colonels' military regime. The palace was constructed in 1878, yet another example of the many fine Athenian buildings designed by architect Ernst Ziller. It was restored in 1935, when it also became home to the Greek Parliament. Although it is closed to the public, it is worth strolling by to see the frontage, the guards on duty outside and, over the wall, a glimpse of the gardens.

➕ 21G ✉ Irodou Attikou ⏲ Closed to the public Ⓜ Syntagma

VOULÍ (NATIONAL PARLIAMENT BUILDING)

The Greek Parliament Buildings stands at the top of Syntagma Square, and its full Greek name is the Voulí ton Ellinon, which literally means the Will of the Greek People. It's a handsome building which was originally built as a royal palace for King Otto, the first King of the modern independent Greek state, and it opened in 1843. It ceased being a royal home in 1924 when the monarchy was first abolished in Greece, and after a period when it was a hospital and then a museum, it became home to the Greek Parliament in 1935. The building is not open to the public, although there are occasional exhibitions in the Parliament Library, and if one is on when you are in Athens you should definitely take the opportunity to look inside, whether you're interested in the subject of the exhibition or not.

➕ 9E ✉ Plateía Syntagmátos ⏲ Closed to the public, except for occasional exhibitions Ⓜ Syntagma

VYZANTINÓ KAI CHRISTIANÍKO MOUSEÍO (BYZANTINE AND CHRISTIAN MUSEUM)

Best places to see, pages 54–55.

a walk around Kolonaki and Lykavitós

From Syntagma Square walk up Vasilissis Sofias, the main road to the left of the National Parliament Building. At the fifth junction on your left, on the corner with Koumbari, stands the Benáki Museum (▶ 44–45).

The museum houses the art collection of a wealthy Greek merchant, Antoine Benáki.

Turn left by the museum, up Koumbari to Kolonaki Square.

Kolonaki is one of the most fashionable districts of Athens, the kind of place where well-to-do Greek ladies walk their dogs. Kolonaki Square is surrounded by designer stores, cafés and smart gift shops.

Cross the square and leave it at the far right corner along the main road, Patriarchou Ioakim. Cross two junctions; at the third, at the first set of traffic lights, turn left up Ploutarchou.

This steep street leads towards Lycabettus Hill (➤ 42–43), visible at the top.

At the end of Ploutarchou you may appreciate taking the funicular to the top of Lycabettus Hill.

Enjoy the views over Athens: on a clear day you can see as far as the island of Aegina (➤ 161).

Take the zigzag path to the left, going down again through the lightly wooded slopes of the hill. If you ignore minor paths to left and right, you emerge on Aristippou, about 100m (110yds) down from the funicular station. Head straight down Loukianou, another steep stepped Kolonáki Street, back down to Vasilissis Sofias, to emerge almost opposite the Byzantine Museum.

Turning left here would take you to the War Museum (➤ 146–147) and, near the Hilton Hotel, the National Gallery (➤ 142). If you have had enough walking for one day, turn right back down Vasilissis Sofias to Syntagma Square.

Distance 3km (2 miles)
Time 1.5 hours without stops, 2–3 hours with stops
Start/end point Plateía Syntágmatos ➕ 8E 🚇 Syntagma
Lunch/tea GB Corner (€€€; ➤ 153)

HOTELS

Achilleas (€)

This reasonably priced hotel is close to Syntagma Square. All rooms have en-suite facilities, air-conditioning and satellite TV.

✉ Lekka 21 ☎ 323-3197; www.achilleashotel.gr 🚇 Syntagma

Andromeda Athens (€€€€)

Situated in a quiet street not far from Lycabettus Hill (➤ 42–43), this luxury hotel is aimed at the business traveller, with computers and fax machines available on request. It was one of the first boutique-style hotels in Athens and has maintained its standards despite the ever-increasing competition.

✉ Timoleondos Vassou 22 ☎ 643-7302; www.andromedahotels.gr 🚌 4

Athens Cypria Hotel (€–€€)

Just off the pedestrianised Ermou shopping street and convenient for the Syntagma Square Metro, the Athens Cypria is an excellent mid-range choice for both price and location. Many of its 71-rooms have balconies, and some of the upper floors have views of the Acropolis – ask when booking. Some luxury rooms have a jacuzzi.

✉ Diomias 5 ☎ 323-8034; www.athenscypria.com 🚇 Syntagma

Athens Hilton (€€€€)

Here you'll get typical Hilton high standards, with a gym, spa and several bars and restaurants, including the stunning Galaxy Roof Restaurant. The hotel is convenient for Syntagma Square (➤ 52–53), the Benáki Museum (➤ 44–45) and the National Gallery (➤ 142), but a bit of a walk from the Plaka.

✉ Vasilissis Sofias 46 ☎ 728-000; www.athens.hilton.com
🚇 Evangelismos

Grande Bretagne (€€€€)

This is Athens' landmark hotel, where the guest register reads like a roll-call of history (➤ 53). It's right on Syntagma Square and features include marbled interiors, swimming pool, spa, top restaurants, city views and impeccable service.

✉ Plateía Syntagmatos ☎ 333-0000; www.grandebretagne.gr 🚇 Syntagma

King George Palace (€€€)

The King George Palace rivals its neighbour the Grande Bretagne as one of the city's top hotels. Renovation has produced top-class facilities such as the acclaimed Tudor Hall restaurant (➤ 155), T Palace bar (➤ 157) and Palace Spa.

✉ Plateía Syntagmatos ☎ 322-2210; www.classicalhotels.com
Ⓜ Syntagma

RESTAURANTS

Boschetto (€€€)

This delightful Italian place is in Evangelismos Park on the edge of Kolonaki and serves fashionable food and fresh pasta, using ingredients popular in both Greece and Italy: squid, spinach, courgettes and cheese.

✉ Alsos Evanelismos ☎ 721-0893; www.boschetto.gr Ⓒ Mon–Sat, lunch, dinner. Closed lunch in winter, two weeks in Aug Ⓜ Evangelismos

Filippou (€€)

Filippou has been serving traditional taverna food to Kolonaki locals since 1923, and despite gentrification of the neighbourhood, it's as popular as ever – and as good.

✉ Xenokratous 19 ☎ 721-6390 Ⓒ Mon–Sat lunch, Mon–Fri dinner
Ⓜ Evangelismos

GB Corner (€€€)

Part of the Grande Bretagne Hotel (➤ opposite), this smart restaurant with piano bar serves a mix of traditional Greek cuisine and continental cooking. You get good food, good service and it's not over-priced.

✉ Grande Bretagne Hotel, Syntagma Square ☎ 333-0000 Ⓒ Daily 7am–1am Ⓜ Syntagma

Gerofinikas (€€)

This smart, secluded place is one contender for the best food in Athens, with a strong Middle Eastern influence showing through in its use of lamb, chicken, yoghurt, spices, nuts and rich desserts.

✉ Pindarou 10 ☎ 362-2719 Ⓒ Daily 12–11:30. Closed public hols

L'Abreuvoir (€€€)

This costly upmarket French restaurant in Kolonaki, where Pavarotti and other celebrities have dined, has elegant decor and equally elegant food – steaks a speciality – plus an extensive and expensive wine list.

✉ Xenokratous 51 ☎ 722-9061 ⏲ Daily lunch, dinner Ⓜ Syntagma

Milos (€€€)

The Hilton is one of the city's best hotels, and the Milos one of its best restaurants. Seafood is the speciality, but they're equally adept with steaks, while one house special is deep-fried courgette and aubergine served with *tzatziki*.

✉ Hilton Hotel, Vasilissis Sofias 48 ☎ 724-4400 ⏲ Daily lunch and dinner Ⓜ Evangelismos

Mona Lisa (€€)

The Mona Lisa can be found in a romantic setting hidden away in Kolonaki. Ambitious pasta and fish dishes are a speciality, served with typical Italian hospitality.

✉ Loukianou 36 ☎ 724-7283 ⏲ Daily lunch, dinner Ⓜ Syntagma

Orizontes (€€€)

At last Lycabettus Hill has got the restaurant that its setting deserves. Take the funicular up to Orizontes and you will be rewarded with spectacular views from the top of the hill, and equally spectacular food. Dishes such as tzatziki risotto have gained it a lot of justifiable attention from Athenian diners.

✉ Lycabettus Hill ☎ 722-7065 ⏲ Daily lunch, dinner Ⓜ Evangelismos

Papadakis (€€–€€€)

Having made her name with a very successful restaurant on the island of Paros, chef Argyro Mbarmbarigou moved to Athens and has been equally aclaimed here for her fresh seafood dishes. Try the octopus salad.

✉ Fokilidou 15 ☎ 360-8621 ⏲ Mon–Sat lunch and dinner Ⓜ Evangelismos

Prunier (€€)

This French bistro near the Hilton Hotel offers a romantic setting in three rooms and typical bistro dishes, such as *coq au vin* and *escargots*. There are more exotic choices on the menu, like quail in oregano and lemon sauce.

✉ Ipsilantou 63 ☎ 722-7379 🕐 Mon–Sat dinner. Closed Jun–Aug 🚌 234

To Kafeneio (€€–€€€)

Don't be fooled by the name, this is no cheap Greek *kafeneion*. It's a smart but relaxed restaurant serving excellent Greek specialities, such as spinach pie, baked aubergines with cheese, and chicken in lemon sauce to international diners, some from the nearby embassies.

✉ Loukianou 26 ☎ 722-9056 🕐 Mon–Sat lunch, dinner. Closed Aug 🚇 Evangelismos

Tudor Hall (€€€)

Fine dining doesn't come any better than this – on the 7th floor of the King George Palace Hotel, with views of the Acropolis. Chef Athanasios Tzanetos trains four times a year with Alain Ducasse, who works with him on the menus. Duck cooked on a spit, served with creamy polenta and fennel with orange, is just one dish.

✉ King George Palace Hotel, Plateía Syntagmatos ☎ 322-2210 🕐 Mon–Sat breakfast, lunch, dinner; Sun breakfast only 🚇 Syntagma

SHOPPING

ANTIQUES, ARTS AND CRAFTS
EOMMEX

This co-operative specialises in handmade rugs produced on traditional looms by weavers from all over Greece.

✉ Metropóleos 9 ☎ 323-0408

Riza

Not cheap, but sells fine examples of hand-made lace, as well as more affordable machine-produced work, glassware and other items from contemporary Greek craftspeople.

✉ Voukourestiou 35 ☎ 361-1157

BOOKS
Pantelides

This is probably the biggest English-language bookshop in Athens, with a knowledgeable owner and stock ranging from popular blockbusting paperbacks to obscure specialist works. There's a good section covering books about Greece, plus dictionaries, art books, cookery and history books.

✉ Amerikis 11 ☎ 362-3673

FASHION
Bettina

This stylish store in Kolonaki stocks some of the best designs by Greek names that can add an extra touch of exclusivity to buying a designer dress.

✉ Pindarou 40 ☎ 323-8759; http://bettina.com.gr

DKNY

Donna Karan's famous New York fashion label offers bold designs and chic but wearable style.

✉ Solonos 8 ☎ 360-3775

JEWELLERY
Elena Votsi

Elena Votsi was already a well-known Greek jewellery designer, but shot to fame in 2003 when she was asked to design a new medal for the 2004 Olympic Games. It was so well received that her design for the front will remain unchanged for future Olympics. You can buy some of her original designs here at her own Athens store in Kolonaki.

✉ Xanthou 7 ☎ 360-0936; www.elenavotsi.com

Zolotas

One of Greece's leading jewellers, and even if you can't afford the items, the jewellery is worth seeing in its own right.

✉ Stadiou 9 ☎ 322-1222

ENTERTAINMENT

BAR
T Palace
This new bar has its own entrance alongside the King George Palace Hotel. A casual place to have a drink or a snack during the day, at night it becomes one of the fashionable hang-outs around Syntagma.

✉ King George Palace Hotel, Syntagma Square ☎ 322-2210

CLASSICAL AND ARTS
The Greek National Opera
Their established home is at the Olympia Theatre along Akadimias, but the company also puts on ballet performances here.

✉ Akadimias 59 ☎ 361-2461; www.nationalopera.gr

Mégaron Athens Concert Hall
This bright building was opened in 1991 and presents ballet, opera and classical music, including performances by the Athens State Orchestra and visiting companies.

✉ Vasilissis Sofias and Kokkali ☎ 728-2000

Pallas Theatre
A venue for major rock concerts, but it also stages some classical performances.

✉ Voukourestiou 1 ☎ 322-4434

JAZZ
Jazz Club Diva
This smart and relaxed venue is well located in the heart of the action in Kolonaki.

✉ Tsokha 43 ☎ 729-0322

REMBETIKA CLUB
Rembetiki Astoria
In a neoclassical building in Kolonaki, this appeals to a more intellectual audience.

✉ Ippokratous 181 ☎ 642-4937

Excursions

If you are only making a weekend visit to Athens you may want to limit yourself to the city itself, though an evening bus ride to romantic Cape Sounion (➤ 162–163) is easily done, and Piraeus (➤ 174–175) and Kifissia (➤ 168) are on the metro. With a few more days, though, there are many other exciting options, available as one- or two-day tours through hotels and travel agents; alternatively, most are equally easy to arrange for yourself.

Those who have never visited a Greek island should certainly take the opportunity. The nearest major island, Aegina (➤ opposite), is only 40 minutes away by the high-speed catamaran. Athens is also the hub of the excellent Greek bus network, with cheap and regular services to famous places such as Mycenae (➤ 172), Epidaurus (➤ 166–167) and the incomparable Delphi (➤ 164–165).

AÍGINA (AEGINA)

Aegina is a popular weekend retreat for Athenians so it can be very busy, especially in high summer. In addition to its proximity, it owes its popularity to the fact that it is quite a green island, with some good beaches, and an exceptional temple – the Temple of Aphaia, which was built in about 490BC and is regarded as one of the best-preserved Doric temples in Greece.

The temple is easy to reach as there are regular buses from Aegina Town, while a visit booked through a travel agent will certainly include a trip to it. The temple is about 60 years older than the Parthenon, and equally impressively set, on a pine-covered hill. If visibility is good and you have binoculars, you can see the Acropolis (► 38–39) from here, as well as the Temple of Poseidon at Cape Sounion (► 162).

Near by is the bustling port and resort of Agía Marina. If you especially want to visit the temple some of the ferries from Piraeus stop here, as well as at Aegina Town, so check first. Agía Marina is a busy package holiday resort, and the island's capital, Aegina Town, has far more of an authentic Greek feel to it. There are some fine old buildings dating from the time when this was the capital of Greece (1826–28), after the War of Independence. The resort also features some interesting churches, the house where the novelist, poet and dramatist Nikos Kazantzakis (1883–1957) wrote *Zorba the Greek*, a small museum, and good waterfront fish tavernas.

🍴 Cafés/restaurants (€) in Agía Marina 🚌 Bus from Aegina Town to Agía Marina stops at the temple

Temple of Aphaia

✉ 0297-32398 🕐 Temple: Mon–Fri 8:30–7, Sat–Sun 8:30–3; site museum open daily 8:30–1. Both closed public hols 💷 Expensive

ÁKRA SOÚNIO (CAPE SOUNION)

The most dramatic way to see Cape Sounion for the first time is from the Athens coastal road: turn a bend and suddenly, in the distance, the magnificent white ruins of the Temple of Poseidon can be seen standing proudly at the tip of the cape on top of the 60m high headland. In actuality, when you get close, you see that the marble is grey (it was mined 5km/3 miles away at Agrileza).

It is easy to get to and from the Cape by bus from central Athens, and a popular time to make the journey is in the late afternoon or early evening, in order to be there for the sunset. A spectacular sunset is not guaranteed, but they are frequent and there can be few more splendid sights than to watch the temple turning into a silhouette against the red sky over the Aegean. The

large island due west is Aegina (► 161), and beyond that is the
east coast of the Peloponnese. To the east is Kea, the closest of
the Cycladic Islands.

The temple was built in 444BC on the foundations of another
building which has been dated back to 490BC. The temple originally
had 34 columns, but only 15 remain standing today. One of these
bears the scratched initials of the English poet and Grecophile,
Lord Byron, who visited here in 1810, though the temple is now
roped off to help preserve it from any modern-day attempts at
adding graffiti.

✉ 22920-39363 🕐 Daily 9:30–sunset. Closed public hols 🖐 Moderate
🍴 Restaurants near by (€€) 🚌 Sounion bus, no number, leaves from
Mavromateon terminal

DELFOÍ (DELPHI)

The ancient Greeks thought Delphi the centre of the world, and anyone visiting the site today will understand why. It has an indisputable atmosphere and an impressive setting between high cliffs and a vast valley of olive trees which falls away below you.

Pilgrims visited the Oracles at Delphi from roughly the 12th century BC to the 4th century AD, to seek advice on all kinds of subjects. The most famous of all the Oracles was the Sibyl, whose rock can still be seen today at the side of the Sacred Way, which winds from the entrance up to the remains of the Temple of Apollo.

The temple ruins date from the 4th century BC, as does the 5,000-seat theatre behind. Climb to the top row of the theatre for one of the best views over the site and down the valley. Above here is a well-preserved stadium and near by is also a superb museum.

You can reach Delphi by public bus, but there are also many organised day trips, bookable through travel agents.

✉ Site and museum: 22650-82312 🕑 Site and museum: Mon 12–6:30, Tue–Sun 7:30–6:30 👋 Expensive 🍴 In village of Delphi
🚌 Delphi bus daily from bus terminal at Liossion 260

EPÍDAVROS (EPIDAURUS)

The ancient theatre at Epidaurus is the finest in Greece, for its setting, its state of preservation and its acoustics. It is said that you can hear a pin drop on the stage from the top of the 55 rows of seats.

The theatre was built in the 4th century BC but only discovered at the end of the 19th century. It was finally restored in 1954. It can seat 14,000 and is still in use for an annual drama festival held in July and August.

Spectators look out over the site of Epidauros, which was dedicated to the healing God Asklepios, the son of Apollo. The site has the remains of a guesthouse, bath, gymnasium and sanctuary buildings, although many are overgrown. The site museum contains a good collection of statues, including some of Asklepios, and a partial reconstruction of the Tholos or rotunda.

☎ Site and museum: 27530-22009 🕐 Site and museum: daily 8–7 (closes 5pm in winter). Closed public hols ✋ Expensive 🚌 Daily from bus terminal at Kifissou 100

KIFISIÁ (KIFISSIA)

This fashionable suburb, at the northern end of the Metro line which runs from Piraeus, has long been an enviable address in Athens. At 276m (905ft), the cooler climate of the area attracts the wealthier citizens, as a glance at the choice of high-street shops will indicate. The town is an attractive and easy day out for the visitor too. From the Kifissia Metro stop you can hail one of the horse-drawn carriages for a tour around the area, with its many grand mansions. Alternatively, simply walk up through the park, cross the busy road and continue on up, perhaps pausing on the left to sample the delights at Varsos, said to be the oldest of Athens' many *zaharoplasteions* (pastry shops). A left turn at the next junction takes you to the **Goulandris Natural History Museum,** a small but impressive collection, which concentrates on the flora and fauna of Greece. It is especially good on birds, butterflies, sea shells and environmental problems. The herbarium alone is said to contain over 250,000 specimens.

🚇 Kifissia

Goulandris Natural History Museum

✉ Levidou 13 ☎ 801-5870; www.gnhm.gr 🕓 Mon–Sat 9–2:30, Sun 10–2:30. Closed Aug 💷 Moderate 🍴 Café (€)

KÓRINTHOS (CORINTH)

It is a pity that the modern town of Kórinthos is not more appealing, for on its doorstep the visitor can see the site of Ancient Corinth, the looming hilltop ruins of Acrocorinth and one of the wonders of the modern world – the Corinth Canal. It is true that the last of these will not detain you long, but it should not be missed, for it is a beautiful, as well as a brilliant, engineering achievement. It is almost 6.5km (4 miles) long and 90m (295ft) high but only 27m (88ft) across, making it unsuitable for many of today's supertankers.

Acrocorinth was also a startling engineering feat in its day. This ancient acropolis has walls that run for 2km (1.2 miles) on top of the hill which dominates the surrounding plain and the Gulf of Corinth. Inside the walls are the remains of further fortifications, houses, mosques and churches, and the views from here are extraordinary.

Down below is the site of Ancient Corinth, once the Roman capital of Greece, with a population of 300,000, supported by a further 460,000 slaves. It also had a great reputation for licentious living, so St Paul's Epistles to the Corinthians were particularly relevant. The well-preserved remains and the Archaeological Museum on the site help the visitor to visualise the city as it was (apart from the bawdy behaviour). The most noticeable building here is the Temple of Apollo, which dates from the 6th century BC, making it one of the oldest of the many temples to be found in Greece.

☎ Site and museum: 2741-31207 🕓 Corinth: daily 8:30–7 in summer, 8–5 in winter. Acrocorinth: daily 8–7 in summer, 8:30–3 in winter. Both closed public hols 🖐 Corinth expensive; Acrocorinth free

MYKÍNES (MYCENAE)

'I have gazed upon the face of Agamemnon,' claimed German archaeologist Heinrich Schliemann to the King of Greece when he unearthed a golden mask on this site. This and other stunning golden treasures are on display in the National Archaeological Museum in Athens (➤ 40–41). Agamemnon's palace or not – and later carbon-dating suggests not – the ruins are still among the most famous and popular in Greece. Few visitors will not experience a thrill when seeing for the first time the famous Lion Gate (c1250BC), almost as familiar an image of Greece as the Parthenon. Beyond the Gate, on the right, is the Royal Cemetery where the golden treasures were found. Near by is the Treasury of Atreus, a simple but superbly striking royal burial tomb.

☎ 27510-76585 🕓 Daily 8–7:30 (winter 8:30–5). Closed public hols
🖐 Expensive 🚌 Take Náfplio bus and ask for Mycenae

NÁFPLIO

Náfplio is far from being the largest place in the Peloponnese – that distinction goes to the port of Pátra, Greece's third largest city – but it is certainly one of the most attractive. Indeed, many Greeks regard it as the prettiest town in the whole of Greece.

There are several reasons for its charm. It looks like a Greek island port, clustered at the base of a headland dominated by not one but two fortresses. Its streets are old and narrow, with Italianate balconies which are flower-filled in summer. It has an immensely attractive large, open, traffic-free main square, while across its attractive harbour can be seen the mountain peaks of the rest of the Peloponnese.

Náfplio is also very cosmopolitan for a small town, attracting artists and craftsmen, and with the daily papers of the world available in several of its shops. It has a range of very good eating places, a small beach and easy access to important ancient sites such as Mycenae, Tiryns and Epídavros. It also has a unique place in Greece's modern history, for it was Náfplio, not Athens, which was the first capital of modern Greece. The country's first President, Kapodistrias, lived and was assassinated here.

Its history is reflected in the two main fortresses and several museums, including an **archaeological museum** with some fascinating items. Little wonder that Náfplio is such a popular spot for Athenians who want a holiday, or simply a short break from the city – it is a mere two hours' drive away.

🍴 Café, restaurants (€–€€€) in town 🚌 Several daily from bus terminal at Kifissou 100

Archaeological Museum

✉ Plateía Syntagmatos ☎ 27520-27502 🕐 Tue–Sun, 8:30–3. Closed public hols 👋 Moderate

PEIRAÍAS (PIRAEUS)

Piraeus is easily accessible from central Athens, being at the end of the Metro line, though its charms are limited. Imagine the traffic of Athens and then add the bustle of one of the Mediterranean's busiest ports. Nevertheless, it can be worth a trip out on a Sunday morning when the flea-market operates in the streets behind the Metro/railway station. It is part of the street life that recalls the award-winning 1959 film, *Never on Sunday*, starring Melina Mercouri as a Piraeus prostitute with the proverbial heart of gold.

It was near the magnificent cathedral of Ágia Triadha, on Filonos, behind the Town Hall, that workmen in 1959 found the impressive bronze statues which form the principal reason for visiting Piraeus's **Archaeological Museum.** The exhibits in the first hall were found in 1930–31 in a sunken ship that had been bound for Italy and which was discovered in Piraeus harbour.

Turn left out of the museum entrance and walk straight down the main street to the Limin Zeas harbour. Turn right here and a short way along the front, across the street, is the **Naval Museum** of Greece. This includes model ships, from ancient triremes to modern-day battleships, and displays covering some of the great naval battles in Greek waters, such as the Battle of Salamis, along with numerous documents and drawings, letters and relics.

The Mikrolimano harbour in Piraeus is also the place where Athenians go to find the best fish tavernas for a leisurely summer Sunday lunch or evening meal.

Piraeus is a sprawling port with two small harbours and one very large one. If you're not familiar with it and you plan to visit an island, it is vital to check in advance, on a map, where your boat leaves from, and how best to get there. For the Argo-Saronic islands mentioned in this guide, ferries leave from Akti Possidhonios and further round the same quay along Akti Miaouli. Hydrofoils for the Saronic islands leave from close by on Akti Tselepi on the east side of the harbour. All docks are only a short walk from the main metro station.

Archaeological Museum

✉ Harilaou Trikoupi 31 ☎ 452-1598 🕙 Tue–Sun 8:30–3. Closed public hols
👆 Moderate 🚇 Piraeus

Naval Museum

✉ Akti Themistokleous ☎ 451-6264 🕙 Tue–Sat 9–2. Closed public hols
👆 Inexpensive 🚇 Piraeus

PÓROS

A visit to Póros gets you two islands for the price of one. Two separate small islands are joined by a causeway. You are also just 400m (440yds) from the mainland across the passage or ford (*póros*) that gives the island its name. Only an hour from Athens, Póros gets as busy as the other Argo-Saronic islands. For a lovely escape, cross to the mainland and walk to the lemon groves of

Limonodhassos, where 30,000 trees perfume the air and paths meander through the groves up to a small taverna serving fresh lemon juice.

Back in Póros Town it's also possible to meander through some of its narrow back streets, to visit the town's small Archaeological Museum, or sit in the waterfront cafés and tavernas watching boats and people come and go. In the interior of the island you can see the scant remains of a 6th-century Temple to Poseidon, but Póros is more a place for enjoying modern holiday life than for the ancient past.

✉ Tourist Police: on the waterfront
✉ 22980-22462 🕙 May–Sep daily

SPÉTSES

Spétses is the Argo-Saronic island furthest from Athens, but it can still be reached in little over two hours on one of the high-speed ferries. It's less expensive than Hydra, has better beaches than Póros or Hydra, is relatively green (its name is a corruption of the Greek word for 'piney') and is just as popular as all the other islands, despite the distance involved!

Spétses became renowned in the late 1960s as the setting for the cult novel by British author John Fowles, *The Magus*, which was later filmed. Fowles lived and taught here and renamed it Phraxos in his novel. The factual Spétses town has, like Hydra Town, many handsome 18th-century mansions built on the strength of its wealthy merchant shipping fleets. One of the finest, built in 1795, now houses the island's museum and is worth a visit. Spétses' charm is enhanced by a partial ban on cars and a good reputation for eating places.

✉ Tourist Police: Botassi ☎ Tourist Police: 22980-73100 ⓘ Museum Tue–Sun 8:30–2:30 ✋ Museum: moderate

ÝDRA (HYDRA)

If you only have time to visit one Greek island while staying in Athens, there are reasons both for and against choosing Hydra. It takes only a little over 90 minutes to reach on the high-speed ferry, and when you arrive the harbour looks so extraordinarily beautiful that you will see at once why people fall in love with the Greek islands. On the other hand, a great many people have already fallen in love with Hydra so it can be extremely crowded. It is also not a typically Greek island – but then every island is different, which is part of their charm.

Hydra was colonized by a crowd of Bohemian artists in the 1960s, and became a very fashionable place to live and to visit, with more than a touch of St Tropez about it. Many of the old mansions lining the harbour were sensitively renovated, returning them to the glory of the days when Hydra had a large merchant shipping fleet that created its 18th-century wealth. Today, very strict building controls and a ban on cars ensure that the island retains its beauty, though there are, of course, constant commercial pressures to ease the restrictions.

You can escape the crowds and fashionable boutiques by walking to one of the island's fishing villages, or heading up above the town for an hour or so to the convent of Ágia Efpraxia and neighbouring monastery of Profitis Ilias, all a welcome return to a more traditional Greek island life.

✉ Tourist Police: Votsi, Hydra Town ☎ Tourist Police: 22980-52205
🕐 May–Oct daily 9am–10pm

HOTELS

AÍGINA (AEGINA)
Aeginitiko Archontiko (€)
Located in a restored traditional mansion, which was first built in 1820, this hotel is stronger on atmosphere than on the quality of its rooms. But it represents a perfectly acceptable and economic option and is conveniently placed in the centre of Aegina Town.
✉ Eakou 1 ☎ 22970-24968

ÁKRA SOÚNIO (CAPE SOUNION)
Grecotel Cape Sounio (€€€)
Superb 5-star hotel with its own restaurant, pools and beach, and perfect views of the Temple of Poseidon. The rooms blend well into the surrounding countryside, on the edge of a pine forest.
✉ Cape Sounion ☎ 22920-69700

DELFOÍ (DELPHI)
Hotel Vouzas (€€)
Just a short walk from the historic site, the Vouzas also provides wonderful views of the surrounding countryside that can be enjoyed from the balcony of your room.
✉ Frederikis 1 ☎ 22650-82232

MIKÍNES (MYCENAE)
La Belle Helene (€)
This is the long-established hotel in which the archaeologist Heinrich Schliemann stayed while excavating Mycenae, up the road. It is simple but clean, with eight rooms, none of them en suite, but its terrific character makes up for the basic amenities.
✉ Mykínes ☎ 27510-62257

NÁFPLIO
Byron (€)
Named after the poet, this intimate hotel is in a back street, opposite the entrance to Ágios Spyridon church. It has 13 rooms, all with a bath, and lots of personality.
✉ Plateía Ágiou Spiridona ☎ 27520-22351; www.byronhotel.gr

PEIRAÍAS (PIRAEUS)
Ideal (€)
The Ideal is handy for the international ferry ports. It has 31 en-suite rooms, phones and air-conditioning. It's worth booking ahead if you need to spend a night in Piraeus.

✉ Notara 142 ☎ 451-1727 🚇 Piraeus

PÓROS
Hotel Seven Brothers (€)
Situated in a little square just off the seafront, the Hotel Seven Brothers has small, simply furnished rooms, each with a balcony and fridge. Ideal for those who require a good budget option.

✉ Póros Town ☎ 22980-23412; www.7brothers.gr 🕐 Call ahead for winter opening

SPÉTSES
Zoe's Club (€€)
A resort complex that is based around some old buildings as well as new ones. Only five minutes' walk from the port, it has its own pool with sea views and rooms well-equipped for self-catering.

✉ Spetses Town ☎ 22980-74447; www.zoesclub.gr

ÝDRA (HYDRA)
Bratsera (€€)
If you've ever felt the urge to stay in a former sponge factory, then be sure not to miss this opportunity. The Bratsera is an excellent conversion, featuring traditional island decor, swimming pool and garden dining area; and it's close to the main harbour.

✉ Tombazi ☎ 22980-53971; www.bratserahotel.com

RESTAURANTS

AÍGINA (AEGINA)
Maridaki (€)
Lively waterfront restaurant-café where you can dine cheaply on salads or omelettes, moderately on grilled octopus or moussaka, or expensively on fresh fish, caught off Aígina that morning.

✉ Dimokratias 6 ☎ 22970-25869 🕐 Daily 8am–midnight

ÁKRA SOÚNIO (CAPE SOUNION)

Ilias (€€)

An alternative to the places outside the Temple of Poseidon is this fish taverna on the beach below. Less impressive view, but slightly cheaper. No surprises on the menu, but lots of good fresh fish.

✉ Ákra Soúnio ☎ 22920-39114 🕐 Daily lunch, dinner 🚌 Sounion bus

DELFOÍ (DELPHI)

Iniochos (€€)

This highly recommended restaurant has superb views over the valley and a very good, varied menu in a town where poor tourist fare is the norm. The menu ranges from mussels and fresh fish to lamb in pastry and several vegetarian options.

✉ Frederikis 19 ☎ 22650-82710 🕐 Daily lunch, dinner

KIFISIÁ (KIFISSIA)

Vardis (€€€)

In the Pentelikon Hotel is this elegant, costly, but good-quality French restaurant serving lobster, *filet mignon*, a range of other meat dishes and salads. Evening pianist.

✉ Deligianni 66 ☎ 023-0650 🕐 Daily lunch, dinner 🚇 Kifisia

MIKÍNES (MYCENAE)

La Belle Helene (€€)

Eat here for a sense of place, as the restaurant is in the hotel Schliemann stayed in while excavating the site (▶ 178). There are no surprises on the menu, but the food is better than – if slightly pricier than – the many tourist-trap tavernas that abound.

☎ 27510-76225 🕐 Daily lunch, dinner. Phone to check if open before going in the evening

NÁFPLIO

Kakanarakis (€)

In a town where many tavernas are aimed purely at the tourist, this excellent place offers Greek specials even out of season: rabbit with feta, or squid in a wine sauce are just two examples.

✉ Vasilissis Olgas 18 ☎ 27520-25371 🕐 Daily lunch, dinner

PEIRAÍAS (PIRAEUS)

Dourambeis (€€€)

One of the best in Piraeus, the Dourambeis is a simple restaurant but with outstanding – and expensive – fresh fish dishes from the Aegean islands, including a delicious crayfish soup.

✉ Athena Dilaveri 29 ☎ 412-2092 🕐 Mon–Sat 8:30pm–1am. Closed Aug 🚇 Piraeus

Kollias (€€)

This renowned Piraeus fish restaurant offers friendly service and inspired cooking.

✉ Stratigou Plastira 3 ☎ 462-9620 🕐 Mon–Sat lunch, dinner. Closed Aug 🚇 Piraeus

PÓROS

Caravella (€)

This waterfront taverna offers a typical, but well-prepared Greek menu.

✉ Paralia ☎ 22980-23666 🕐 Daily lunch, dinner

SPÉTSES

Exedra (€)

Right on the harbour, this is one of the best of Spétses' many fine restaurants. It concentrates on fish, which it cooks it with flair, and the menu includes a delicious shrimp, lobster and feta cheese bake, plus many vegetarian options.

✉ Old Harbour ☎ 22980-73497 🕐 Daily lunch, dinner

ÝDRA (HYDRA)

Xeri Elia (€)

Tucked down a narrow street, this traditional taverna with a garden area, offers simple but beautifully prepared meat and fish dishes, including lobster.

✉ Off main square ☎ 22980-52886 🕐 Daily lunch, dinner in summer, weekends in winter

Index

Street Index

Acknowledgements

The Automobile Association would like to thank the following photographers, companies and picture libraries for their assistance in the preparation of this book.

Abbreviations for the picture credits are as follows – (t) top; (b) bottom; (c) centre; (l) left; (r) right; (AA) AA World Travel Library.

4l Anafiótika, Plaka, AA/A Mockford and N Bonetti; **4c** Sunset over Ýdra Town, AA/P Wilson; **4r** View towards Acropolis, AA/A Mockford and N Bonetti; **5l** Marina, Bay of Mikrolimano in Piraeus, AA/P Wilson; **5c** Odeon of Herodes Atticus, Acropolis, AA/T Harris; **5r** Delphi, AA/T Harris; **6/7** Anafiótika Plaka, AA/A Mockford and N Bonetti; **8/9** View across Athens from Pnýka, AA/A Mockford and N Bonetti; **10/11** Art Shop, Plaka, AA/A Mockford and N Bonetti; **10c** Parthenon at night, AA/A Mockford and N Bonetti; **10bl** View of Keramikos, AA/A Mockford and N Bonetti; **10br** Modern Olympic Complex, Athens, AA/A Mockford and N Bonetti; **11c** Organ grinder, Plaka, AA/A Mockford and N Bonetti; **11b** Scattered Ruins, Agorá, AA/A Mockford & N Bonetti; **12/13t** Food for sale, Athens, AA/A Mockford and N Bonetti; **12** Feta cheese, AA/A Mockford and N Bonetti; **13** Taverna, Plaka, AA/A Mockford and N Bonetti; **14t** Olive oil, AA/A Mockford and N Bonetti; **14b** Pistachio nuts for sale, AA/A Mockford and N Bonetti; **15** Brettos Ouzerie, Plaka, AA/A Mockford and N Bonetti; **16/17t** Sculpture by Anna Chromy, National Archaeological Museum, AA/A Mockford and N Bonetti; **16/17b** Street in Monastiraki, AA/A Mockford and N Bonetti; **17** Taverna, Plaka, AA/A Mockford and N Bonetti; **18t** Retsina, AA/P Wilson; **18/19** Ágioi Apóstoli Church, Agora, AA/A Mockford and N Bonetti; **19** Ouzo for sale, AA/A Mockford and N Bonetti; **20/21** Sunset over Ýdra Town, AA/P Wilson; **26** Tram, Syntagma Square, Athens, AA/A Mockford and N Bonetti; **27** Taxis, Athens, AA/A Mockford and N Bonetti; **28/29** Trolley bus, Syntagma Square, Athens, AA/A Mockford and N Bonetti; **29** Telephone boxes, AA/A Mockford and N Bonetti; **31** Traffic policeman, Athens, AA/A Mockford and N Bonetti; **32** Metro station sign, AA/A Mockford and N Bonetti; **34/35** View of Panathenaic Way, towards Acropolis, AA/A Mockford and N Bonetti; **36/37t** View of Monastiraki, Roman Agorá, AA/A Mockford and N Bonetti; **36/37b** Columns of the Stoa of Attalos, Agora, AA/A Mockford & N Bonetti; **37t** Ágioi Apóstoli Church, Agora, AA/A Mockford and N Bonetti; **37b** Statue of Hadrian, Agorá, Athens, AA/A Mockford and N Bonetti; **38** Eréchtheion, Acropolis, AA/A Mockford and N Bonetti; **38/39t** View across Acropolis from Pnýka, AA/A Mockford and N Bonetti; **38/39b** Temple of Athena Nike, Acropolis, AA/A Mockford and N Bonetti; **40/41** Sculpture by Anna Chromy, National Archaeological Museum, AA/A Mockford and N Bonetti; **41t** Sculpted Head, National Archaeological Museum AA/T Harris; **41c** Artifact from Santorini, National Archaeological Museum, AA/P Wilson; **42** View from Areopagos Hill, AA/A Mockford and N Bonetti; **42/43** View from Lycabettus Hill, AA/A Mockford and N Bonetti; **43** View to Lycabettus Hill, AA/A Mockford and N Bonetti; **44** Benáki Museum, general view inside, AA/A Mockford and N Bonetti; **45t** Benáki Museum, café area, Benáki Museum; **45c** Inside Benáki Museum, Benáki Museum; **45b** Painted Chest Detail, Benáki Museum, AA/A Mockford and N Bonetti; **46c** Museum of Cycladic Art, AA/A Mockford and N Bonetti; **46b** Inside the Museum of Cycladic Art, AA/A Mockford and N Bonetti; **47** Entrance to the Museum of Cycladic Art, AA/A Mockford and N Bonetti; **48** View from Lycabettus Hill, AA/A Mockford and N Bonetti; **48/49** Olympic Stadium, Ardhittos Hill, AA/P Wilson; **50** Flea market, Monastiraki, AA/A Mockford and N Bonetti; **50/51** Ceramic Collection, Museum of Greek Folk Art, AA/A Mockford and N Bonetti; **52c** Syntagma Square, Athens, AA/A Mockford and N Bonetti; **52b** Parliament Building, Syntagma Square, Athens, AA/A Mockford and N Bonetti; **52/53** Changing of the Guard at the Tomb of the Unknown Soldier, Syntagma Square, AA/A Mockford and N Bonetti; **54** Byzantine Museum, AA/P Wilson; **54/55** Detail of Vierge Hodigitria, Byzantine Museum, AA/P Wilson; **55** Icon, Byzantine Museum, AA/R Strange; **56/57** Marina, Bay of Mikrolimano in Piraeus, AA/P Wilson; **58/59** People relaxing, taverna, Athens, AA/P Wilson; **60/61** Harbour, Rafna, AA/T Harris; **62/63** Children street painting, Plaka, AA/A Mockford and N Bonetti; **64** View of Panathenaic way, towards Acropolis, AA/A Mockford and N Bonetti; **65** Temple of Olympian Zeus from Acropolis, AA/A Mockford and N Bonetti; **66/67** View from Lycabettus Hill, AA/A Mockford and N Bonetti; **68/69** Traditional costumes, Benáki Museum, AA/A Mockford and N Bonetti; **70t** Dolmades, AA/A Mockford and N Bonetti; **70b** Saganaki, Athens, AA/A Mockford and N Bonetti; **71** Greek salad and saganaki, Athens, AA/A Mockford and N Bonetti; **72/73** Roman Odeon of Herodes Atticus, Acropolis, AA/T Harris; **75** National Gardens in Athens, AA/A Mockford and N Bonetti; **76/77t** Monument to Filopappou, Hill of the Muses, Acropolis, AA/T Harris; **76/77t** Odeon of Herodes Atticus, AA/A Mockford and N Bonetti; **78** Ilias Lalounis Jewellery Museum, AA/A Mockford and N Bonetti;

Sight locator index

This index relates to the maps on the covers. We have given map references to the main sights in the book.

Dear Reader

Your comments, opinions and recommendations are very important to us. Please help us to improve our travel guides by taking a few minutes to complete this simple questionnaire.

You do not need a stamp (unless posted outside the UK). If you do not want to cut this page from your guide, then photocopy it or write your answers on a plain sheet of paper.

Send to: **The Editor, AA World Travel Guides, FREEPOST SCE 4598, Basingstoke RG21 4GY.**

Your recommendations...

We always encourage readers' recommendations for restaurants, nightlife or shopping – if your recommendation is used in the next edition of the guide, we will send you a **FREE AA Guide** of your choice from this series. Please state below the establishment name, location and your reasons for recommending it.

_____
_____
_____
_____
_____

Please send me **AA Guide** _____

About this guide...

Which title did you buy?

AA _____

Where did you buy it?_____

When? <u>m m</u> / <u>y y</u>

Why did you choose this guide? _____

_____
_____
_____
_____

Did this guide meet your expectations?

Exceeded ☐   Met all ☐   Met most ☐   Fell below ☐

Were there any aspects of this guide that you particularly liked? _____

_____
_____
_____

continued on next page...

Is there anything we could have done better? _____

_____

_____

_____

About you...

Name (*Mr/Mrs/Ms*) _____

Address _____

_____

_____ Postcode _____

Daytime tel nos _____

Email _____

Please only give us your mobile phone number or email if you wish to hear from us about
other products and services from the AA and partners by text or mms, or email.

Which age group are you in?
Under 25 ☐   25–34 ☐   35–44 ☐   45–54 ☐   55–64 ☐   65+ ☐

How many trips do you make a year?
Less than one ☐   One ☐   Two ☐   Three or more ☐

Are you an AA member? Yes ☐   No ☐

About your trip...

When did you book? m m / y y   When did you travel? m m / y y

How long did you stay? _____

Was it for business or leisure? _____

Did you buy any other travel guides for your trip? _____

If yes, which ones? _____

_____

_____

Thank you for taking the time to complete this questionnaire. Please send it to us as soon as
possible, and remember, you do not need a stamp (*unless posted outside the UK*).

_____

| **AA** Travel Insurance call 0800 072 4168 or visit www.theAA.com |

_____